WHO ARE THE PEOPLE OF CANADA ANYWAY?

WHO ARE THE PEOPLE OF CANADA ANYWAY?

Waiting for the Next Referendum

by "Citizen X"

eastendbooks
Toronto 1997

Printed in Canada by Metrolitho

Editor: Nadine Stoikoff
Photograph on cover: © Glenn Lewis
Cover design: Andy Tong

Canadian Cataloguing in Publication Data

Citizen X
    Who are the people of Canada, anyway? : waiting for the next referendum

Includes bibliographical references and index.
ISBN 1-896973-02-7

1. Canada – Politics and government – 1993- .* 2. Regionalism – Canada.
3. Federal-provincial relations – Canada.* 4. Canada – English-French relations.
I. Title.

FC635.C57   1997   971.064'8   C97-932005-4
F1034.2.C57   1997

eastendbooks is an imprint of Venture Press
45 Fernwood Park Avenue
Toronto, Canada
M4E 3E9
(416) 691-6816 [telephone]
(416) 691-2414 [fax]

Contents

One
Why I'm Confused
7

Two
Why French Kissing Hasn't Worked
37

Three
Why the Loyalists Were Wrong and the Fur Traders Were Right
57

Four
The Maple Leaf Rag
(An interlude)
79

Five
Jobs, Jobs, Jobs
(Another interlude)
93

Six
Why Everyone Hates Ontario
(and the anglophone minority in Quebec)
113

Seven
The Death of the National Business Class
(and why it may not be such a bad thing)
133

Eight
Who Are the People of Canada, Anyway?
149

Nine
Let's Just Do It and Get It Over With
(An immodest proposal)
179

Ten
How to Survive if Nothing Happens at All
213

Index
235

One

WHY I'M CONFUSED

1

La belle province

What most impressed my father about the first referendum was just how many people in Quebec did vote Yes, even then. That was in May 1980, which doesn't seem so long ago to me. But I know it's ancient history to my three sons – at the beginnings of their own adult lives, in a world I wish I'd never left myself.

It seems there are no choices about time. It just moves on, indifferent to what any of us may want. I remember turning thirteen, in the suburbs in the late 1950s, and thinking I'd be happy if I never got a day older. At that point, all I knew was that Quebec was "la belle province," where a lot of people spoke French. About five years later, in the summer of 1963, two high-school friends and I hitch-hiked to Percé, on the Gaspé coast.

Remembering the FLQ

A few days ago I was talking to a younger business acquaintance over the phone. He said he'd just come back from a six-week trip to Thailand. Making conversation, I said it must have been quite something. Even in this new age of troubled Asian economic miracles, he said that it made him appreciate just how lucky he was to be living in Canada. Then he said that he guessed it had been a lifetime experience all the same.

Looking back now, that trip to the Gaspé in the summer of 1963 was a kind of lifetime experience for me. I still have vivid images of it in my mind. Most of them are stronger than anything I remember about later trips outside the country. I can still see "FLQ" in big white letters, painted on great stretches of rock along the banks of the St. Lawrence. At one point we hitched a ride with a guy who claimed to have loaned a tent to an FLQ fugitive, in flight from the law.

Now, when I look up **Front de libération du Québec (FLQ)** in *The Canadian Encyclopedia*, I see that it was "founded in March 1963." A few months later "underground FLQ activists (some of whom were arrested) placed bombs in mailboxes in 3 federal armories and in Westmount, a wealthy upper-middle-class anglophone area of Montréal."

I must have had some knowledge of this when I went to the Gaspé, in the summer of 1963, from the newspapers and my family's primitive black-and-white television set. But today, I have to consult the encyclopedia to get the details straight.

What's remained in my mind is the image of the big white letters on the stretches of rock, resting beside several other, gentler memories: drinking quart bottles of cold Dow ale on a sunny hillside, at the edge of a convent, not far from the actual town of Gaspé – watching nuns in grey habits doing some type of farm work in the convent fields.

A few years later, I was haphazardly listening to the radio, in an apartment in the city in "the rest of the country" where I have always lived. Paul Gérin-Lajoie, whose name was vaguely familiar to me from university classes I was supposed to be attending, was talking (in English) about the quiet revolution in Quebec. All I recall about the radio program now is a feeling it gave me: that what was happening in Quebec was somehow fascinating. Since then the feeling has twisted and turned inside me, in various directions. But the fascination has never quite left.

French Canada dreaming in the 1960s

Of course, hardly anyone is really fascinated by Quebec today, even, it sometimes seems, in Quebec. Hardly anyone is fascinated by anything today. Who can be fascinated by balancing the budget, even if it does (or some now say did) need to be done?

Globalization, viewed deeply enough, can be rather interesting, and it is certainly vast and dramatic. But it is all very abstract. It lacks the romantic fascination of the FLQ, up there on the rock in big white letters, on the way to the Gaspé coast. And even in the distinctively Canadian version of anglo North America in the 1960s – the real global village in which I grew up – the mere name "Paul Gérin-Lajoie" could have an exotic appeal.

In fact, I think that what fascination I can still find in the *neverendum* great debate on the future of Canada and Quebec goes straight to its roots in the time of my own youth. What happened to the dreams of the 1960s? The Quebec sovereigntist movement is one of them, and it's in imminent danger of coming true (well, maybe ... more or less).

It almost seems to be a rule of politics that the closer dreams actually do come to coming true, the more boring or even worse they become. My children's generation, it sometimes distresses me to think, have learned this rule from mine. And that's one reason why younger people today are not at all as interested in politics as they were in the 1960s.

The 1976 triumph of René Lévesque

From the start, the romantic, terrorist, and ultimately murderous FLQ had been accompanied by the more sensible Quebec Liberal Party of the quiet revolution – run by the likes of Jean Lesage and Paul Gérin-Lajoie, and for a time even René Lévesque.

Yet, for those who wanted the romance of a sovereign or independent French-speaking Quebec without terrorism, at first there was also the left-wing Rassemblement pour l'indépendance nationale (RIN). In 1964 the fiery orator, Pierre Bourgault, became its leader. In the 1966 Quebec provincial election, the RIN won 6% of the popular vote. For those who just wanted the romance of nationalism in an older sense, there was the former federal Créditise, Gilles Grégoire, and the right-wing Ralliement National (RN). It picked up another 3% of the vote in 1966.

Then René Lévesque bolted from the Quebec Liberal Party and formed the Mouvement souveraineté-association (MSA) in 1967 (elsewhere, the centennial year of the Canadian confederation). In 1968 the MSA, the RIN, and the RN joined together to form the Parti Québécois (PQ), under the leadership of Lévesque. In the same year Pierre Trudeau, the immaculately bilingual native son of Montreal, became leader of the federal Liberal Party and prime minister of Canada.

In 1970 the terrorist FLQ kidnapped the British trade commissioner in Montreal, murdered the Quebec Liberal cabinet minister, Pierre Laporte, prompted the "October Crisis" and Pierre Trudeau's midnight roundup of suspicious francophone radicals, and then faded from public view. Then on November 15,

1976 (I have just looked up the exact date), René Lévesque and the Parti Québécois won a Quebec provincial election – a mere eight years after the PQ's founding in 1968: an impressive feat, technically, no matter what else you may think.

I happened to be in Montreal, on a brief holiday with my wife, when the PQ won. I have a recollection of standing in the train station on what must have been the 16th of November, looking at the headlines in the papers. I was starting to realize that my youth was over, forever, and that I would actually grow old like everyone else. I had children of my own, a steady job, a mortgage, and hardly any time to think about anything.

Even in November 1976, however, what was happening in Quebec still seemed quite fascinating to me. But from here, a long and increasingly more tedious journey set in. Now, more than twenty years later, in the wake of the second sovereignty referendum, in October 1995 (and the rather odd, low-turnout Canadian federal election in June 1997), I am much less fascinated, and much more confused. Of course, it's important to keep your sense of humour about all this. Canada is a place that works best with a sense of humour. Sometimes I think Canadians, whoever they may be, are far too serious about Canada. Other times I think we are not at all serious enough.

Exhibit 1
Canada and Its Provinces and Territories
Geographic Area and Population, 1996

	Area, land, and freshwater (km², 000s)	Population (000s)	Population as % of all Canada
Quebec	1,541	7,139	24.7
Rest of Canada	8,430	21,708	75.3
Ontario	1,069	10,754	37.3
British Columbia	948	3,724	12.9
Alberta	661	2,697	9.3
Manitoba	650	1,114	3.9
Saskatchewan	652	990	3.4
Nova Scotia	55	909	3.2
New Brunswick	73	738	2.6
Newfoundland	406	552	1.9
Prince Edward Island	6	135	0.5
Northwest Territories	3,426	64	0.2
Yukon Territory	483	31	0.1
CANADA	9,971	28,847	100.0

SOURCE: Statistics Canada.

12

2

My Uncle and the Draft Legal Text

I like to look at the world from the bottom, to start from what's actually down on the ground. It's the most democratic approach, and (in theory at least) I'm relentlessly democratic.

I do think the global village is real in some important ways. Right now, it seems to me, all the old cultures of the world are dying or being transformed into something new. And they all have their own legacies for the global future. Democracy – as both an ideal and a kind of partial achievement – is the greatest legacy of the old culture from which I descend myself.

Family ties

That, in any event, is how it seems to me. I'm not really sure why. It probably has something to do with being young in the 1960s. Yet, to take just the cases down on the ground that I know best, my brother and sister were young in the 1960s too. But they don't think as I do about these things.

All three of us, as best as I can tell, share sentimental attachments to Canada – the "northern North American" new country that is not really a country, or at least not yet. This no doubt has a lot to do with our various parents and step-parents, and aunts and uncles, and all that (some of whom were born in old countries, but came to Canada when they were very young).

My brother, however, is not too interested in politics. Though broad-minded in his own way, he is more attached than I am to what I see as the dying old culture from which we both descend. He went into business more aggressively than I did, and has done quite well. And he has never shared even my early fascination with the sovereigntist movement or anything else in Quebec.

My sister (or, to be technical, my half-sister), Veronica, has lived in Ottawa for many years now, with a supposedly important federal civil servant named Ted. She is interested in Quebec, but not in the sovereigntist movement. In her youth she fell in love, from a distance, with bilingualism and Pierre Trudeau. I am slightly more familiar with the French language than my brother. But Veronica can carry on extended conversations in French.

Veronica also believes that democracy is just a convenient illusion. Like my brother (and some other people I know), she thinks my view of the world is just naive. My ultimate response to this criticism is that, at the very bottom of everything, it is not me but my sister and my brother and so forth who are just naive.

In fact my brother, who is so different from me in most respects, sometimes does seem to grasp how seminally realistic I can be. Several years ago, during a period of experimentation with his computers, he passed on a copy of an old photograph of me, taken not too long after I had returned from my trip to the Gaspé. It was a shot from the shoulders up. Just above my hairline he had typed in large bold letters: **"The future's in my head ..."**. Of course he meant it sarcastically, as a joke. But I framed it, anyway, and hung it up on a wall in my house.

Politics on television

I doubt that my brother has paid much attention to what happened in Quebec after the Parti Québécois election victory in November 1976. I can only remember one real conversation with him on the subject over the past few decades. He was sceptical about almost everything that had anything to do with Quebec.

Veronica, living in Ottawa, has been much more intimately involved, but in a very partisan way. She has been an aggressive rest of the country. Though she has always been close to my brother, she once told me that she "learned long ago never to talk with him about politics, and especially politics in Quebec."

For me, the continuing saga of Canada and Quebec since November 1976 has been mostly an endless television series that periodically gets cancelled but then returns, again and again.

I read the newspapers as well, and I buy books. (My wife tells me that there are far too many books in our house. Every now and then, I build new bookcases. My ideal would be to have a house that looked a lot like a library.) In the past few years, my sons have guided me through the mysteries of the Internet. And my wife and I usually visit Veronica and Ted in Ottawa a few times a year. I listen to the radio, occasionally, on the weekend. But, as I say, for me the never-ending Canadian debate has mostly been something that I've watched on TV. Nowadays we have a thirty-five-inch set in a room upstairs, with videotapes in bookcases on either side.

From the 1980 referendum to the troubled waters of Meech Lake

It was on television that I followed the first Quebec sovereignty referendum, in May 1980, with its long and tortuous question about "sovereignty association." The result was 40.5% Yes and 59.5% No. René Lévesque and the sovereigntists lost. But my father can't have been the only person in the rest of the country who was surprised that they did as well as they did.

Then Pierre Trudeau "patriated" the original Canadian federal constitution from the United Kingdom and added a Charter of Rights and Freedoms, which referred to "English and French" as "the official languages of Canada," and was accompanied by some further talk about the "existing aboriginal and treaty rights of the aboriginal peoples of Canada." I remember watching the official ceremonies in Ottawa on TV, in April 1982.

At the same time, though René Lévesque and the Parti Québécois had lost the 1980 referendum, they had won another Quebec provincial election in April 1981. Unlike the governments of all the other provinces, the PQ government of Quebec would not sign Trudeau's new Constitution Act, 1982. And this finally led to the Meech Lake Accord of 1987.

I still have a video of Trudeau on television, marked "May 29, June 3, 1987." He's telling the late Barbara Frum why he is against the Meech Lake Accord. By this time, however, Brian Mulroney had succeeded Trudeau as prime minister of Canada.

Under the Meech Lake Accord, the provincial government of Quebec (now managed by Robert Bourassa and the Quebec Liberal Party) agreed to sign the 1982 "new constitution," in exchange for the "recognition that Quebec constitutes within Canada a distinct society." The Accord was cast as another amendment to the original Canadian federal constitution (formerly the British North America Act, and now called the Constitution Act, 1867).

I remember talking briefly with Veronica over the phone when all this happened, in the spring of 1987. But I was busy with my own life, and didn't pay a lot of attention. Though Mulroney and the provincial premiers had agreed to Meech Lake, it was still subject to ratification by the legislatures of all ten provinces, over the next three years. And as time wore on, many other people who hadn't paid much attention started to think about Canada (or so it seemed to me). My television set spouted a lot of confusion. My own fascination with what was happening in Quebec twisted into a tangle of strange emotions.

Trudeau had tried to make new room for French Canadians and the French language in Canada at large, as an *alternative* to René Lévesque's sovereignty inside the predominantly French-speaking province of Quebec. Meech Lake tried to implement somewhat blunted versions of the Trudeau and Lévesque solutions *together*. (What francophone Quebec really wanted, the comedian Yvon Deschamps had quipped in 1981, was "an independent Quebec in a united Canada.") As Trudeau explained to Barbara Frum in 1987, he had always believed that this could never work, because it would ultimately be perceived as unjust by the English-speaking majority in the rest of the country.

In any case, by June 1990 the legislatures of Manitoba and Newfoundland had still not ratified the 1987 agreement among Mulroney and the premiers. The francophone media in Quebec (and my sister, Veronica) cast Clyde Wells of Newfoundland as the villain. In the rest of the country, the *Maclean's* magazine "man of the year" was the Cree member of the Manitoba legislature, Elijah Harper, who had held up a white feather, to signal the death of the Meech Lake Accord.

Charlottetown, O Charlottetown

As you may not exactly want to remember, the failure of the Meech Lake Accord in 1990 led to the failure of the Charlottetown Accord in 1992.

The theory here was that Meech Lake had not won enough

popular support in Canada at large because it concentrated too much on the problems of Quebec, and not enough on the rest of the country. And by this point, I had started to pay particular attention myself (still hoping that I could somehow regain my youthful fascination with what was happening in Quebec).

According to newspaper clippings I collected at the time, in the Charlottetown Accord Quebec's distinct society was watered down and accompanied by: **[i]** a watered-down version of "Senate reform," supposedly to please western and Atlantic Canada; **[ii]** a less watered-down version of "aboriginal self-government," supposedly to please the descendants of the original inhabitants of the present Canadian territory; and **[iii]** various watered-down versions of various other things (women's rights, multiculturalism, etc.), supposedly to please everyone else.

This time, the federal government and all ten provincial governments (eventually including Quebec, still under the management of Robert Bourassa and the Quebec Liberal Party) reached agreement – along with the two territorial governments and representatives of four different aboriginal organizations. For greater democratic certainty, however, the Charlottetown Accord was submitted to a popular referendum in which the entire country participated, from coast to coast to coast. And, of course, I voted too, just after supper, in an old Anglican church gymnasium a few blocks from my house.

Not settling the issue, once and for all

The question here was very short. It just asked voters whether they agreed that "the Constitution of Canada should be renewed on the basis of the agreement reached on August 28, 1992?"

To appreciate what this meant you had to know something about the agreement reached on August 28. But there was a deluge of information in the media and the mail. Copies of the twenty-eight-page Final Text of the Consensus Report On the Constitution, dated August 28, 1992, and a fifty-one-page Draft Legal Text, dated October 9, 1992, were widely available before the vote on October 26.

You could say: Right. Who would ever look at these things?

Yet at some point that October, my brother and I had gone to visit an aging uncle, at his flat over a store. Usually, he read magazines about cars and boats. But the Draft Legal Text was on his coffee table. There were jam stains on the cover and the pages had been manhandled, like one of his car magazines.

In the end the Charlottetown Accord didn't work any better than Meech Lake. In the October 26 referendum only 44.5% of the Canada-wide electorate voted Yes. In Quebec, 55.3% voted No. The agreement was rejected even more strongly in Alberta, Manitoba, and especially British Columbia.

My guess is that my uncle, having completed his manhandling of the Draft Legal Text, finally voted with the Canada-wide majority. But I'm fairly certain that my brother, my sister, and I all wound up on the losing side (though without any deep sense of disappointment).

Despite her earlier attachments to Pierre Trudeau, Veronica made it clear that she would vote Yes from the start. Just after we left my uncle's flat that October, my brother had referred himself to the rare document on the coffee table. He said that his own inclination was to vote No, but that his colleagues at work were urging the importance of voting Yes, to get the issue settled, once and for all. He supposed they were probably right. For what I imagined were different reasons of my own, so did I.

Exhibit 2
Referendum on the Charlottetown Accord, 1992

	% Voting Yes*	% Voting No*
British Columbia	**31.7**	**67.9**
Manitoba	37.8	61.7
Alberta	39.6	60.0
Yukon Territory	43.1	56.3
Quebec	**42.4**	**55.3**
Saskatchewan	44.4	55.1
Nova Scotia	48.4	51.0
Ontario	**49.8**	**49.5**
Northwest Territories	60.2	39.0
New Brunswick	61.3	37.9
Newfoundland	62.9	36.5
Prince Edward Island	73.6	25.8
CANADA	**44.5**	**54.4**

*Discrepancies between Yes and No totals and 100% are accounted for by spoiled ballots.

SOURCE: Elections Canada.

Exhibit 3
Referendum Questions, 1980-1995

Quebec Sovereignty I, 1980 (Quebec only):

The government of Quebec has made public its proposal to negotiate a new agreement with the rest of Canada, based on the equality of nations. This agreement would enable Quebec to acquire exclusive power to make laws, levy taxes and establish relations abroad – in other words, sovereignty – and at the same time to maintain with Canada an economic association including a common currency. No change in political status resulting from these negotiations will be effected without approval by the people through another referendum. On these terms, do you give the government of Quebec the mandate to negotiate the proposed agreement between Quebec and Canada?

Charlottetown Accord, 1992 (All Canada):

Do you agree that the Constitution of Canada should be renewed on the basis of the agreement reached on August 28, 1992?

Quebec Sovereignty II, 1995 (Quebec only):

Do you agree that Quebec should become sovereign, after having made a formal offer to Canada for a new economic and political partnership, within the scope of the bill respecting the future of Quebec and of the agreement signed on June 12, 1995?

In the Rest of the Country

The failure of the Charlottetown Accord, of course, finally led to the second Quebec sovereignty referendum, in October 1995.

By this point, the Parti Québécois, which had lost the provincial elections of 1985 and 1989 to the Quebec Liberal Party, was back in office under the more or less uncompromising sovereigntist, Jacques Parizeau. Lucien Bouchard, a former minister in Brian Mulroney's cabinet at Ottawa, was leader of the PQ's new federal counterpart, the Bloc Québécois. And in the 1995 referendum campaign, Parizeau and Bouchard had the support of Mario Dumont, a former nationalist leader of the Quebec Liberal youth wing.

This time the question was quite short as well (though, as in 1980, addressed only to residents of Quebec). Should Quebec "become sovereign, after having made a formal offer to Canada for a new economic and political partnership?" The vote was held on October 30, and the result was very close: 49.4% Yes, and 50.6% No.

I still have some vivid television memories here. Earlier on in the evening of October 30, before the Montreal polls came in, it looked as if the Yes side might win. For half an hour or so I felt a great resurgence of my youthful fascination about what was happening in Quebec. Maybe the 1990s were going to be just the 1960s turned upside down.

After the second referendum (or is it the third?)

In the end this did not quite happen, and no doubt that was a good thing. Almost immediately, Jacques Parizeau resigned (just after blaming "money and the ethnic vote" for the Yes side's narrow defeat). A few months later, he was officially succeeded as PQ leader and Quebec "premier ministre" by Lucien Bouchard, the new darling of the Québécois.

Bouchard has promised, again and again, that there will indeed be yet another sovereignty referendum in Quebec – and that this time the Yes side will win.

According to present Quebec law, this next referendum cannot take place until another provincial election has been held. And the restrained performance of the Bloc Québécois in the 1997 Canadian federal election may have pushed the dates of both the next Quebec provincial election and any subsequent sovereignty referendum ahead in time. Meanwhile, the present Parti Québécois government has been concentrating on the necessary but increasingly tricky task of balancing the budget.

Bouchard has made clear as well that his own preference is for a sovereign Quebec that will have some kind of new "economic and political partnership" with Canada, or even "the rest of Canada." He has joined all the other provincial premiers and the federal prime minister, Jean Chrétien (resolutely folksy and figurative half-stepson of Pierre Trudeau), on a Team Canada trade mission abroad.

Personally, I think it is somehow significant that Lucien Bouchard's attractive wife, Audrey, is a former airline stewardess from California. I was impressed when, on the day of her husband's official inauguration, early in 1996, she confessed to the television cameras that, as an American, she just didn't have strong opinions about politics in Quebec.

The most radical branches of the PQ itself have apparently come to mistrust Bouchard. Even before the 1997 federal election, there was some softening of support for the sovereigntist cause in Quebec opinion polls. As I've already alluded to, in the 1997 election the Bloc Québécois won a mere 38% of the popular vote.* And subsequent polls have cast still more doubt on the future of the most radical sovereigntist dreams.

The girl with the long auburn hair

My sister, Veronica, reads all this as evidence for the view that there is still hope for "federalism" in Quebec. Though I'm quite sceptical myself, she may be right. But even if she is, it seems to

---

*Sovereigntist partisans also argue, with some reason, that the low turnout in 1997 suggests many sovereigntist voters just stayed home.

me that this is now rather beside the point.

What the very close result of the 1995 Quebec referendum has finally done for me is change the nature of "the future of Canada and Quebec," altogether. And I don't see how it can be changed back to where it was (or where I thought it was).

For half an hour or perhaps even longer, on the evening of October 30, 1995, all of us in the rest of Canada who were watching the results on TV had to contemplate the imminent prospect that Quebec actually would try to secede from the confederation. Despite all that had happened in the preceding thirty years, "we" were not remotely prepared.

Very early in the morning of October 31, still perched on the edge of my couch in the TV room, I felt that my youthful fascination had somehow wandered into another universe. What may or may not happen in Quebec was no longer any business of mine. All that mattered was the rest of the country, where I live myself. Thirty-two years later, my trip to the Gaspé coast had led to my own front door.

I saw Veronica over the 1995 Christmas holidays, and tried to explain my new feelings about the future of Canada and Quebec. Of course, she said I was just playing into the hands of the sovereigntists. Again, she may be right, but it seems to me that this is now beside the point as well.

Veronica did say something else, and it struck closer to my own sense of where the mark really is. We had gone for a quick drink, at a bar in the Byward Market in Ottawa. (My wife and Ted were still dutifully traipsing through an unusually boring exhibition at the National Gallery.)

"You know," Veronica urged at one point, "I think you've probably always felt this way. You were never really fascinated by Quebec. If you had been, you'd have learned to speak French properly. You were just fascinated by the sovereigntist movement in Quebec, because you sensed that it might eventually force you to confront your own feelings about English-speaking Canada. And I think you're going to find that English-speaking Canada is impossible without Quebec."

I didn't know exactly what to say about this at first. I just shrugged my shoulders and looked around the bar. Several tables away I noticed a young couple, speaking French. The girl had beautiful long auburn hair and she was wearing a tight magenta sweater. She was talking with great animation. Her companion stared at her intently, but it seemed to me that he was paying almost no attention to what she said.

I looked at Veronica: "Part of that may be true," I managed to say. "But if it is, Quebec is just as impossible without English-speaking Canada." Veronica, who couldn't see the young couple from where she sat, just looked back at me and rolled her eyes.

Hello lobsters

In fact, I long ago gave up on trying to figure out what the elusive majority in Quebec really thinks (if it knows itself). I do agree that Veronica and her friends are correct when they argue that nothing which approaches a majority in Quebec supports outright "secession" or "separation" or "independence." The questions in *both* the 1980 and 1995 sovereignty referendums talked about some form of continuing "association" or "partnership" between Quebec and the rest of the country.

The trouble here, as best as I can make out, is that once these things get started they take on a life of their own.

Not long after the 1995 referendum, I caught a tape of Jacques Parizeau's unused Yes-side victory speech on TV. He didn't seem to be taking the concept of offering Canada a new partnership seriously at all.

A few weeks before this tape was made, Parizeau had said in public that it didn't matter what Quebec voters thought they were voting for when they voted Yes: once enough of them had done the deed, they'd be like lobsters boiling in the pot of some new and altogether independent country of Quebec. After the 1995 referendum, I read in the papers that a group of Montreal journalists had watched Parizeau's unused Yes-side victory speech together in some vacant TV studio. When it was over, one of them had remarked aloud: "Well, hello lobsters."

And then, as you may remember yourself, during the 1997 federal election campaign Parizeau published a book. And here he revealed that, not long before the 1995 referendum, a noted figure in France had advised him to declare the independence of

Quebec unilaterally, and quickly, if the Yes side actually won.

When all you mean is Canada

With all this in view, part of the difficulty is that it is now undeniably unwise for the rest of the country to *depend* on Quebec for a Canadian future. The sharpest point that the 1995 referendum brought home for me, however, runs deeper still.

October 30, 1995, cast a harsh light on Canada outside Quebec. If you share the sentimental attachments to the place that my brother and sister and I do (despite all our other differences), what you see in this light is hardly encouraging.

If Veronica is right – and English-speaking Canada is in fact impossible without Quebec – then we have at last bumped into the unmistakably serious prospect that "Canada" may be just a piece of history which is about to end.

Of course, it still seems to me quite unlikely that this will actually happen. But no one can credibly dismiss the prospect out of hand any longer, the way Jean Chrétien did, during the months and then weeks just before the October 1995 referendum in Quebec. And once this kind of prospect is right in your face, the way it is now, it changes everything.

Even less encouragingly, my own sense is that as many of us in the rest of the country have begun to look at ourselves in the new harsh light, we have begun to wonder whether Canada has any kind of serious future, regardless of what may or may not happen in Quebec. The rest of Canada has spent so much time worrying about Quebec and French Canada over the past thirty years that it has almost lost track of what *its Canada* is, and where it may or may not be going.

Alas, this points to weaknesses in the rest of the country that cannot ultimately be blamed on francophone Quebec (as convenient as that would be). Yet French-Canadian nationalism has always understood these weaknesses, and played on them skilfully. The play has become so skilful over the past generation that Canada at large is almost played out.

What I'm talking about here cuts a lot deeper than "Senate reform" or "aboriginal self-government" or any of the other items that figured in the Charlottetown Accord of 1992 – as markers for the rest of the country's presumed interests in some new and fairer deal with the distinct society in Quebec.

It cuts right down to the most ancient and fundamental question about English-speaking Canada. Wouldn't it just make a lot more sense if the country outside Quebec were officially part of the all-too-neighbouring United States of America, as it already is in so many different but, as yet, still unofficial ways?

Several years ago, I was working for a client in California with business interests in Canada. Following an old local tradition that I had absorbed from my bookshelves, I referred to Canada as "northern North America," in a document that I sent to Los Angeles. My California client queried back: "Why do you say northern North America when all you mean is Canada?"

I am enough of a North American myself to grasp what was meant. The present population of the largest American state of California is somewhat larger than the entire population of Canada, including Quebec. Population is what counts when all you're thinking about is markets for goods and services. It's reasonable for business interests in California to think of Canada as just another large state of the union (and not even the largest at that). And, as I certainly know myself, in English-speaking Canada we do watch a lot of television made in California.

Back in the USA

In the midst of the great debate on Canada and Quebec, Americanization of this sort received a particular push from the Canada-US Free Trade Agreement of the late 1980s. The FTA took effect on January 1, 1989, and, according to Veronica's lifetime companion, Ted, it's intriguing that the Meech Lake Accord failed during the FTA's early implementation period.

I was neither a strong supporter nor a strong opponent of the FTA. But I agreed with a friend of Ted and Veronica's, who once said, when asked after dinner, that there was "a side of it that's obvious ground for caution and concern, from the standpoint of any serious Canadian political future."

Happily enough, my extensive book collection has persuaded

me that Canada has survived for as long as it has t'
of almost mystical luck or secret strength, that m
flow from some guardian aboriginal Great Spirit. There a.
a few signs that the Great Spirit of Canada is watching over us
even today. And I think you do have to allow that this is, at least,
somewhat encouraging.

Here, in any event, I agree with Ted, who argues that the
sharpest edges of the Canada-US FTA have been significantly
blunted by the 1994 North American Free Trade Agreement
among Canada, the United States, and Mexico.

Politically, we are better off in a trade deal with the US that
includes more partners than the US and ourselves alone. Apparently, this is why Jean Chrétien's federal Liberals, despite earlier
noises to the contrary, finally went along with NAFTA. More
recently, they have struck a related interim trade deal with Chile
– to enhance its potential as the next NAFTA partner.

Personally, I'm inclined to give Chrétien's cynical, but
stalwart, last gasp of the old federal establishment in Ottawa
fairly high marks on this front. The Canadian future today is only
quite, and not altogether, bleak.

Even so, in the wake of the October 1995 referendum in
Quebec, the ancient question of Canadian annexation to the
United States has become a more almost-serious subject in
English-speaking Canada than at any other time I can remember.
Oddly enough, I think this helps explain why so many of us in the
rest of the country are less noticeably upset by the presumed
prospect of Quebec's secession than some federal pundits and
political leaders think we ought to be.

After all, the absolute worst that can happen to any of us is
that we will become citizens of the USA. I don't welcome this
prospect at all myself. Whatever fate may bring, I will remain an
aspiring Canadian until the day I die. But I like the United States
well enough, and I'm quite comfortable there. People in Europe
and other parts of the world, when they see me or hear me talk,
already think I'm an American. Even for me, the prospect of
becoming an American citizen is hardly a fate worse than death.

I am often told as well that I am rather more "into Canada"
than many other people who live in the place. If I feel this way,

ıow must many other people feel?

A few weeks ago, while we were watching television in the room upstairs, I asked my own wife: "Just how would *you* feel if Canada actually were to disappear into the bowels of the USA?" She thought for a moment, and then she said (perhaps because she knew it would irk me – we've been married for a long time): "I wouldn't be all that upset."

Exhibit 4
American States and Canadian Provinces, 1993

Population (000s)

California	31,211	Oklahoma	3,231
New York	18,197	Oregon	3,032
Texas	18,031	Iowa	2,814
Florida	13,679	**ALBERTA**	**2,688**
Pennsylvania	12,048	Mississippi	2,643
Illinois	11,697	Kansas	2,531
Ohio	11,091	Arkansas	2,424
ONTARIO	**10,813**	Utah	1,860
Michigan	9,478	West Virginia	1,820
New Jersey	7,879	New Mexico	1,616
QUEBEC	**7,228**	Nebraska	1,607
North Carolina	6,945	Nevada	1,389
Georgia	6,917	Maine	1,239
Virginia	6,491	Hawaii	1,172
Massachusetts	6,012	**MANITOBA**	**1,125**
Indiana	5,713	New Hampshire	1,125
Washington	5,255	Idaho	1,099
Missouri	5,234	**SASKATCHEWAN**	**1,012**
Tennessee	5,099	Rhode Island	1,000
Wisconsin	5,038	**NOVA SCOTIA**	**931**
Maryland	4,965	Montana	839
Minnesota	4,517	**NEW BRUNSWICK**	**756**
Louisiana	4,295	South Dakota	715
Alabama	4,187	Delaware	700
Arizona	3,936	North Dakota	635
Kentucky	3,789	Alaska	599
South Carolina	3,643	**NEWFOUNDLAND**	**584**
BRITISH COLUMBIA	**3,574**	Vermont	576
Colorado	3,566	Wyoming	470
Connecticut	3,277	**PEI**	**133**

SOURCES: US Bureau of the Census, Statistics Canada.

4

The Geographic Fact

One reason a lot of English-speaking Canadians don't take being Canadian too seriously, I sometimes think, is that it puts you under too much pressure to justify your own existence.

I have an old friend who came to Canada from another place, in his early twenties. I have known him almost from the moment he stepped off the plane. Around the time when the Meech Lake Accord really began to become controversial, we were having a drink after work. At one point he said to me, somewhat impatiently: "What is Canada all about, anyway, besides hockey?"

A very big country

This is exactly the sort of question that makes it a liability to wear whatever Canadian sentiment you might feel on your sleeve. But I tried to respond.

After thinking haphazardly for a bit, I said something to the effect that, whatever else, Canada's greatest asset was that it had a vast amount of geography. Its population was slightly less than the population of the largest American state of California. But, geographically, Canada was the second-largest country in the world (after what was then still known as the USSR). In fact, *geographically, Canada was (and still is) somewhat larger than the entire United States of America.*

My friend was not at all impressed. He seemed to feel that "a vast amount of geography" was not much of an answer to his question. I nonetheless came away from the conversation with some sense of having enlightened myself.

During the 1960s, recognizing the French fact in Canada became the great Canadian crusade. Now that this fact has received its almost definitive political expression in the 1995 Quebec referendum (perhaps), some say we, in the rest of the country, ought to be embarking on another crusade – a bold new quest, as it were, for the French fact's historic alter-ego. And if we ever did such a thing, I think we'd discover that the real

Canadian alter-ego to the French fact is not English-speaking Canada or anything like that. It simply *is* the awesome sweep of the country's vast geography, from coast to coast to coast.

Does Canada really defy geography?

Ted and Veronica are good friends with a historian called Walt, who also lives in Ottawa. Walt's greatest distinction is probably his drop-dead gorgeous wife, Madeleine (who looks a bit like Marilyn Monroe). But when he isn't pondering historical documents or admiring Madeleine, Walt is also a part-time wilderness adventurer. He has seen a lot more of Canada's vast geography than I have. He says it scares and even terrifies people at first, and they turn away from it, in a state of primal fear.

I have been on just enough minor forays into the less remote northern wilderness to sense a little of what he means. Scare and terrify and primal fear, however, are probably somewhat too exaggerated for dramatic effect. By definition, even part-time adventurers are prone to tell tall tales.

In any case, it used to be said that Canada is a country which defies geography. But Walt argues that this flows from a sense of the past which stopped growing somewhere in the 1920s.

Suppose, Walt says, you ask yourself a variation on the question that my friend from another place posed, at the height of the debate on the Meech Lake Accord: "Why does Canada exist today, anyway? Why is it an official member state of the United Nations, with its own national currency and the second-largest national territory in the world?"

According to Walt, if, as you ponder this question, you also happen to ponder what has been learned about Canadian history since the 1920s, the answer is obvious enough. Canada is the result of a historic geographic unity in northern North America, that arose in the sixteenth, seventeenth, and eighteenth centuries, and then acquired the beginnings of the particular political expression we know today in the nineteenth century. In fact, Canada does not defy geography at all. It is a historical creation of geographic facts.

Making love in a canoe

As even Walt concedes, clever people who do have some sense of all this and still do not want to think too much of Canada will point out that *the* Canadian geographic fact *is* strictly historic.

The great wild and romantic key to Canada's geographic unity is that when the vast northern glaciers retreated, at the end of the last ice age, they left behind a lot of water. One result is that in the most northern parts of North America (unlike in the other parts), you can still paddle a canoe all the way from one ocean, to another ocean, to another ocean.

If you are crazy enough to try even a bit of this today, you will find yourself using the ancient northern North American aboriginal transportation technology of the canoe and portage. And, along with the exhausting effort of paddling a canoe, this involves a great deal of stupendously athletic portage (or staggering through the bush with a canoe on your head).

It is historically true that the ancient northern aboriginal canoe and portage remained an economically profitable transportation technology in Canada much further into the nineteenth century than seems quite believable today.

It is also true (and even wild and romantic in its own way) that in the late nineteenth and early twentieth centuries, some of Canada's historic northern transcontinental canoe routes were quite deliberately revived by the Canadian national railway system, in the early industrial age of steam.

Yet, just as the age of the canoe and portage once gave way to the age of the railway (and the telegraph, and mass-production manufacturing, and so forth), at the edge of the twenty-first century the old industrial age of steam is giving way to a new high-technological age of airplanes, and television sets, and electronic computers, and global telecommunications, and virtual reality, and all that. And in this new age, we have begun to reassess all merely historic forms of geographic unity.

Where virtual reality goes wrong

In the midst of this reassessment, there are bold, new voices, urging that the national geography of Canada is no longer important. The history of the future is indifferent to whether or not the present province of Quebec secedes from the present Canadian confederation, because the future of the present confederation cannot possibly be what it was in the past.

I think that certain aspects of this argument do make some sense. Yet some of the boldest voices get carried away. They push their case too far. And when they do, they sound a lot like the apocryphal Newfoundlander, who argues that it will actually be a good thing if Quebec "leaves" Canada, "because it will make the drive to Toronto a lot shorter."*

For one thing, saying that the historic geographic unity of Canada is no longer important immediately raises the question of "important to whom?" I can see how it makes sense to say that, in the new age of virtual reality and the microelectronic revolution, there are certain traditional economic interests to whom the Canadian national geography, created by the canoe and portage, is no longer important. But there are a lot of other things out there on the ground today that would not be where they are if it weren't for Canada's historic geographic unity. And even if it were desirable, I am not at all sure that it is possible for these things to disappear.

Back in the middle of the 1970s, I told an older friend who grew up on a farm in Saskatchewan that, because I had grown up and still lived in a big city, it was hard for me to identify with Canada's vast national geography. More recently, Walt has helped me appreciate that this is quite absurd. The big city I live in at the edge of the twenty-first century is where it is – and to no small extent what it is – because of the "northern North America"

---

*John Crosbie, from Newfoundland, has already told this well-known joke on TV. I assume this means that it is also *not* politically incorrect to put it into print. Or if it is, real people in Newfoundland don't care.

created in the seventeenth, eighteenth, and nineteenth centuries, by the aboriginal technology of the canoe and portage.

Canada's vast geography now belongs to you

To get very quickly to the crucial point, if there is some secret spiritual strength to Canada today (and I certainly hope this is somehow true myself), it lies in the rather odd fact that, haphazardly and almost accidentally, in our own time Canada's historic geographic unity has finally become a democracy.

By definition, every democracy has "a people" (technically, in Canada today, everyone who is legally entitled to vote in a federal election – or in a federal referendum, like the one that was held on the failed Charlottetown Accord). And the key question right now is whether Canada's historic geographic unity is still important to the people of Canada.

My current working hypothesis is that it probably is – even for people like my wife, who enjoy irritating people like me by saying out loud that they wouldn't be all that upset if Canada actually were to disappear into the USA.

The ultimate logic is extremely simple, and it has virtually nothing to do with the Canadian national health care system or anything like that. If you are part of the people of Canada – by birth or by choice or simply because you happen to find yourself residing in the place by accident – then at the very bottom of everything, *Canada's vast geography now belongs to you.*

Even if you just know most of this geography by looking at it on a map, you can easily see that it is, indeed, very vast. And North American that you also are (or have also chosen to become), you can't quite escape the feeling that something quite this enormous must somehow be very valuable.

It may just be an accidental, and even somewhat crazy legacy, from what now seems to be the rather improbable or even crazier age of the canoe and portage. But it involves almost 10 million square kilometres of often quite striking real estate, from the Atlantic, to the Arctic, to the Pacific oceans. It is not something that any sensible person would lightly give up.

Madeleine's objection

And yet, alas, in northern North America life can never be quite so simple. The summer before the 1995 Quebec referendum, Ted and Veronica, Madeleine and Walt, and my wife and I were drinking California wine, on a hot and sunny afternoon in the Gatineau hills. And (with Veronica cheering her on) Madeleine, whose paternal grandmother was born in the sovereigntist hotbed of Jonquière, Quebec, raised some gentle doubts about the whole truth of "Canada's vast geography now belongs to you."

"My grandmother's father," Madeleine said, "could only speak French. And she told me more than once that the Rocky Mountains and all that could mean nothing to him."

And of course, I thought later, Madeleine is right here (as well as irresistible in so many other ways). None of this Canadian national geographic logic makes at all as much sense for French-speaking people of Canada in Quebec as it makes for English-speaking people of Canada in the rest of the country. Even worse, now that Canada's historic geographic unity finally *has* become a democracy, this trouble has turned into what increasingly seems to be an impossible problem.

I'm not sure just what I used to think about this problem. Years ago, on my way to the Gaspé coast, I think I probably thought it was not quite so impossible as it seems to be now. (And I can still understand why people in other places just can't understand why even an unreal country like Canada should have any kind of impossible problems.) But right now, I am quite sure that it is quite confusing. And I, myself, am quite confused.

Exhibit 5
The World's Fifteen Largest National Territories

Country	Area (km^2, 000s)
Russian Federation	17,075
CANADA	**9,971**
China	9,600
United States	9,363
Brazil	8,521
Australia	7,692
India	3,137
Argentina	2,771
Sudan	2,505
Algeria	2,461
Zaire	2,344
Saudi Arabia	2,331
Kalaallit Nunaat (Greenland)*	2,176
Mexico	1,979
Indonesia	1,906

*Technically, still a possession of Denmark, granted "home rule" in 1978.

SOURCES: George Thomas Kurian, *The Book of World Rankings* (1980); *The World Almanac and Book of Facts 1995.*

Two

WHY FRENCH KISSING HASN'T WORKED

5

Île de Montréal

There is more than one way out of a confused space. The easiest is to blame a particular person, and often enough it works.

Today, Pierre Trudeau (or Pierre *Elliott* Trudeau, as Quebec sovereigntists like to stress) is not as famous in either the rest of Canada or Quebec as he used to be. Among people my sons' age he seems to be best known for his ill-fated marriage to the current Margaret Sinclair Trudeau Kemper from Vancouver, British Columbia. I have no doubt at all, however, that he still has something to do with my own confusion.

The virtues of the failed philosopher king

I can honestly report that I was sceptical about Trudeau from the start. But I finally found it impossible not to admire him as well.

In fact I suspect that, even today, quite a few people in all parts of the country would grudgingly allow that Pierre Trudeau is as close as Canada has come to a great national political leader. And I certainly agree with this assessment myself.[*]

This may seem a strange judgement to make about someone who has been largely repudiated by the events of the past decade or so (and especially by the October 1995 referendum in Quebec). Yet great leaders can have virtues, even when they fail.

According to Walt, Trudeau's greatest virtue was that "his sense of the country's past had grown beyond the 1920s." Trudeau had a philosophical passion for the historic geographic unity of Canada. And he tried to bring this passion to bear on the country's public life.

Shortly after he became prime minister of Canada in 1968, he

---

[*]Not long ago, *Maclean's* magazine consulted a group of historians, who ranked William Lyon Mackenzie King as Canada's greatest prime minister. My own reasons for preferring Trudeau should be clear by the end of this book (at which point I will also have a little more to say about Mackenzie King – who, I agree, can be quite fascinating, if you've had enough to drink.)

wrote a characteristically austere foreword to his paddling colleague Eric Morse's short book, *Fur Trade Canoe Routes of Canada: Then and Now*, which appeared "in association with Environment Canada, Parks Canada, and the Canadian Government Publishing Centre."

Walt says that among his fellow wilderness adventurers, this slender volume has since become a minor classic. And in its pages you can still discover the real Canada of Pierre Trudeau. It is the Canada created by the northern aboriginal transportation technology of the canoe and portage, during the multiracial fur-trade romance of the sixteenth, seventeenth, eighteenth, and earlier nineteenth centuries, from coast to coast to coast.

Bilingualism and all that

There was, of course, another key message in the new Canadian gospel according to Trudeau. It is the message a lot of people couldn't help wondering about from the start. And I think it has almost completely lost its way today.

Walt argues that "bilingualism" by itself is probably not an adequate short summary of Trudeau's argument here. There are at least limited references to the use of "Either the English or the French Language" in what is now known as the Constitution Act, 1867. And there was something of a muzzled and now largely forgotten struggle over French language rights outside Quebec, during the earlier history of the 1867 confederation.

Trudeau's real innovation, Walt says, was to link the French fact with the democratization of the geographic fact – in a way that made the theoretical case for some significant degree of English and French bilingualism, throughout Canada's vast geography, almost indisputable in the later twentieth century.

The "mother tongue" of about one-quarter of the people of Canada (inside and outside, though mostly inside Quebec) is French. If democracy means that the country's enormous geography belongs to all the people of Canada, then, in principle, those among the one-quarter of the people whose mother tongue is French ought to be able to live their lives in their mother tongue, anywhere in Canada they choose.

More realistically, if the alluring democratic proposition that "Canada's vast geography now belongs to you" can at least acquire some more or less extensive practical meaning for the "francophone majority" in Quebec, then the false siren calls of the rising sovereigntist movement will fall on deaf ears.

Canada can forget the threat that Quebec will secede and destroy the geographic integrity of the present confederation. It can get on with the more important business of building a real human society, that begins to live up to the country's geographic grandeur and vast extent.

Trudeau and the 1995 referendum

As I say, like a lot of other people in the Canada that existed down on the ground during the late 1960s and early 1970s, I had a certain scepticism about all this from the start. I was impressed by Trudeau's theoretical case for bilingualism. But the English-speaking part of the country in which I live was even less remotely bilingual a generation ago than it is today. I wondered whether my part of Canada could ever become hospitable enough to the French language to make Trudeau's concept of the Canadian future work.

Veronica likes to stress that there *has* been progress in moving towards French and English bilingualism in Canada outside Quebec since the late 1960s. Yet I think the evidence is now almost conclusive that this progress has not been at all close enough to the standards required by Trudeau's vision.

For virtually all practical political purposes, the francophone majority in Quebec is the ultimate arbiter of whether what progress there has been is sufficient. And the most damning result of the October 1995 referendum for Trudeau's argument was that not just 49.4% of all the people of Quebec but *some 60% of the francophone majority voted Yes* to the question: "Do you agree that Quebec should become sovereign ... ?"

Veronica's view here is a variation on my father's view of the May 1980 referendum. What is *really* significant about October 1995, she says, is that 40% of the francophone majority still voted No. I agree that this does mean something. But my own sense is that, whatever may or may not exactly happen in the future, the journalist Richard Gwyn's verdict on the morning after the 1995 referendum will finally prove at least half-correct: "What has died, in fact, is Pierre Trudeau's idea of Canada."

Notes on a native son

The deepest question about Trudeau is still what it was at the start. How could such an intelligent and sophisticated person ever imagine that it would be possible to transform English-speaking Canada into the kind of bilingual society which could stop the sovereigntist movement in Quebec?

The problem here, I think, is that Trudeau's public persona while he was in office was rather misleading. To many of his warmest supporters, he seemed to be breathing the fresh air of some new spirit of global cosmopolitanism. But the key to Trudeau's vision of Canada's future is that he is, at bottom, a confirmed native son of the city of Montreal, where he grew up and still lives today.

Until the middle of the 1970s, Montreal was Canada's most-populous metropolitan region. Until the 1950s, many in other parts of the country would have agreed that it was Canada's economic capital as well. Still more to the point, when Pierre Trudeau was growing up in Montreal, it was the only big city in Canada (and almost the only place of any sort) with the practical makings of a real bilingual society, down on the ground where most people live. Trudeau, himself, with his French father and Scottish mother, was a unique creation of at least one side of Montreal's bicultural urban scene.

I find Montreal deeply intriguing myself. One of my three sons has gone to university there. (Another has gone to university in Toronto, and another in Vancouver.) I always look forward to visiting the place, and I know it much better now than I did when I was younger. I sometimes think that if I had grown up on the same street as Pierre Trudeau, I might feel that the prospect of an authentically bilingual Canadian society, from coast to coast to coast, was somewhat less hopelessly wild and utopian than I actually think it is today.

Alas, the rest of Canada (and even *the rest of Quebec*) is just not and never can be quite like Montreal. When I say this to Veronica, she starts talking about "monumental parochialism." Yet when you get right down to it, Pierre Trudeau is just as monumentally parochial as everyone else. At the height of the debate on the Meech Lake Accord, I caught an interview with the historian Robert Bothwell on TV. And he summarized what now seems to me the most relevant side of the argument, in a mere dozen words. The trouble with Trudeau is that "he sees Canada from one end of Montreal Island to the other."

Exhibit 6
Trudeau's National Geography

(*from his Foreword to Eric Morse,* Fur Trade Canoe Routes of Canada: Then and Now, *1969*)

In the past the teaching of history in our schools has been dominated by traditions inherited from Europe. On that continent history has been filled with battles, and the lives of national heroes. In Canada we have had few decisive battles and not many dominant leaders. Much more important to our history has been the struggle of nameless Canadians to improve their lives in our often hostile environment. This struggle has produced its share of adventures and heroism.

But perhaps this lesson is best learned outside the classroom. Anyone who wishes to get a feeling for the unique history and geography of this country can do no better than follow Eric Morse's example. All who do will derive a double pleasure from this book: the pleasure of reading it and the pleasure of exploring some of the routes it describes. Like those of us who have canoed with the author, I am sure they will come to share his enthusiasm for the tough but satisfying life of the voyageurs.

Exhibit 7
Canada and Its Provinces and Territories
Percent Population by Mother Tongue, 1991

	% English (Anglophone)	% Other (Allophone)	% French (Francophone)
Quebec	**9.2**	**8.8**	**82.0**
Rest of Canada	**77.7**	**17.5**	**4.8**
New Brunswick	64.6	1.4	34.0
Ontario	74.6	20.4	5.0
Manitoba	73.5	21.8	4.7
Prince Edward Island	94.3	1.2	4.5
Nova Scotia	93.3	2.5	4.2
Yukon Territory	88.7	8.0	3.3
Northwest Territories	55.2	42.3	2.5
Alberta	81.2	16.5	2.3
Saskatchewan	83.3	14.5	2.2
British Columbia	78.9	19.5	1.6
Newfoundland	98.6	0.9	0.5
CANADA	**60.4**	**15.3**	**24.3**

SOURCE: Statistics Canada.

6

All Alone by the Allophone

Language statistics have been one of the great banes of what has passed for Canadian public life during the last few decades. But I spend a lot of time looking at all kinds of statistics in my ordinary work. And, as Veronica's companion Ted likes to say, "they have advantages in the complex world we inhabit today."

Language statistics in Canada help clarify just how enormous the challenge of Pierre Trudeau's bilingual vision has been. They can also help you put your finger on stubborn facts that often get lost in the blur of day-to-day public debate.

Mother tongue

There are two types of statistics that bear directly on the running Canadian sore of language differences. And it only adds to the confusion if you don't keep both of them in mind.

You can start to see this if you try to put some numbers on the phrase "francophone majority in Quebec." The statistics most frequently reported in the media on this subject are for a concept called "mother tongue," or "the first language learned which is still understood at the time of the census." Three classes of mother tongue are particularly relevant: French, English, and Other (or as it is said in French – and often enough in Canadian English – francophone, anglophone, and allophone).

On this definition, some 82% of all the people in Quebec (as of the 1991 federal census) report that their mother tongue is French.[*] This is the largest measure of the francophone majority in Quebec. And it is the one typically alluded to by the Parti Québécois and the sovereigntist movement. When it is said that some 60% of the francophone majority in Quebec voted Yes in the 1995 referendum, this is the definition that is meant.

On this same definition, just under 5% of all people in the rest

---

[*]Historically, this proportion has also been quite stable, all the way back to the nineteenth century.

of Canada at large reported their mother tongue as French in the 1991 census. Among all provinces and territories outside Quebec, only New Brunswick has a significantly higher percentage.

The key statistic here is mildly dramatic: some 34% of the New Brunswick population was francophone in this sense in 1991. Though this has something to do with the province's present geographic proximity to Quebec, its deepest roots lie in the troubled history of ancient Acadia – the French-speaking region of the present Canadian Atlantic provinces. (In the middle of the eighteenth century, some "Acadiens" were shipped by the conquering British empire to what is now Louisiana, where they became the Cajuns of the present-day USA.)

A related key wrinkle is that because Ontario has a much larger total population than New Brunswick, its 5% francophone statistic translates into a much larger absolute number of people than the 34% francophone statistic in New Brunswick. Almost entirely because of its present geographic proximity to Quebec, *Ontario has the largest absolute number of people reporting their mother tongue as French outside Quebec* (just over half a million people in 1991, compared with about half that number in New Brunswick). And this has been a favourite Canadian language statistic of Pierre Trudeau and his various supporters.

Knowledge of official languages

These mother-tongue statistics do give some broad sense of the numerical dimensions of the French and English issue in Canada today. If they are all you look at, however, you will likely still be more confused about why the Quebec sovereigntist movement has proved so potent over the past three decades than you actually need to be. There is another approach to measuring or numerically expressing the francophone majority in Quebec. And it gets much closer to the real strength of the Parti Québécois.

The statistics here deal with "knowledge of official languages" – or the languages that people can actually speak (or think they can speak) at the time of the census. Again, there are three particularly relevant classes: French only (or unilingual francophone), English only (unilingual anglophone), and both

English and French (or bilingual).

From this angle (and, once more, as of the 1991 federal census) there is a "francophone majority in Quebec," not only in the sense that some 82% of the population has a French mother tongue, but also in the much more decisive and politically pregnant sense that *French is the only language which some 58% of the Quebec population knows how to speak.*

According to Veronica's lifetime companion Ted, people from the United States who inadvertently take a rare interest in Canada are often astounded to discover that the majority of people in Quebec actually cannot speak English. And I'd guess that more than a few people in Canada outside Quebec are also only vaguely aware of this rather poignant statistic, at best. Even after hitch-hiking through assorted unilingual-francophone places on my way to the Gaspé, well over thirty years ago, it is only in the more recent past that Ted has prompted me to look up the hard data on this branch of the subject myself.

The sheer enormity of the challenge to Trudeau's vision

We can perhaps all be forgiven for our collective ignorance in some degree. As Ted also points out, for various strategic reasons the unilingual francophone majority in Quebec is not something that any of the official parties to the debate on the future of Canada and Quebec has wanted to talk about very much. And for Canadian federalists in the style of Pierre Trudeau, the 58% of the Quebec population that only speaks French makes the quite enormous extent of the practical bilingual challenge in the rest of the country all too painfully clear.

The unilingual francophone majority in Quebec is no less a part of the people of Canada than any other fraction of the Canadian population. If the alluring democratic proposition that "Canada's vast geography now belongs to you" is going to have practical meaning for unilingual francophones, then some quite substantial percentages of the people in the rest of the country are going to have to speak French. Otherwise, unilingual francophone Quebecers are going to have no one to talk with, as they take advantage of the vast geography that also belongs to them, from the Atlantic, to the Arctic, to the Pacific oceans.

Yet, as the 1991 federal census also makes clear, *just under 88% of the population in Canada outside Quebec (and more than 90% in five of the nine provinces involved) only know how to speak English.* And while the bilingual population in Canada outside Quebec has increased by more than 40% between 1961 and 1991, even today only some 10% of the population in the rest of the country even claims to speak French.

A lot of subtle and thorny things could be said here. But in the end, I think, the chief practical trouble is that, largely as a result of sheer demographic pressure, it is just so much easier to learn English in Quebec than it is to learn French in the rest of the country. Thus, the Canadian official bilingualism pioneered by Pierre Trudeau's federal regime in Ottawa, from 1968 to 1984, has created anglophone politicians and civil servants in the federal capital city who speak French with varying degrees of skill. It has made the federal bureaucracy a more hospitable place for Quebec francophones. And it sometimes seems to have created a new unwritten convention of the Canadian constitution, to the effect that the office of prime minister of Canada must now be filled by a bilingual resident of Quebec. But it has not, in any remotely significant degree, improved the traditionally dismal prospects of any brave unilingual francophone Quebecers, who dare to explore their future as Canadians in Canada outside Quebec.

Exhibit 8
Canada and Its Provinces
Unilingual Population, 1991

% Population reporting knowledge of only one official language		
	% French	% English
Newfoundland	0.0	96.5
Saskatchewan	0.0	94.2
Alberta	0.1	92.1
British Columbia	0.0	91.6
Nova Scotia	0.2	91.1
Prince Edward Island	0.2	89.6
Manitoba	0.2	89.4
Ontario	0.5	86.1
New Brunswick	12.5	57.9
Quebec	**58.1**	**5.5**
CANADA	15.5	67.1
Rest of Canada	**0.7**	**87.9**

SOURCE: Statistics Canada.

Exhibit 9
Canada and Its Provinces
Bilingual Population, 1961, 1991

% Population reporting knowledge of both English and French		
	1961	1991
Quebec	25.5	35.4
New Brunswick	19.0	29.5
Ontario	7.9	11.4
Prince Edward Island	7.6	10.1
Manitoba	7.4	9.2
Nova Scotia	6.1	8.6
Alberta	4.3	6.6
British Columbia	3.5	6.4
Saskatchewan	4.5	5.2
Newfoundland	1.2	3.3
CANADA	**12.2**	**16.3**
Rest of Canada	**6.9**	**9.8**

SOURCE: Statistics Canada.

A Footnote on la conquête

In 1967, shortly before he became prime minister, Trudeau explained in the foreword to a book of his essays that long ago "I had already made up my mind to swim against the tide."

As best as I can make out, by the time he left office in 1984 more than a few people, outside *and* inside Quebec, had begun to ponder just how enormous the Canadian tide that he had ultimately wound up trying to swim against actually was.

"We don't want you to speak French"

About half a dozen years after Trudeau's resignation, at some point during the last dying weeks of the Meech Lake Accord, I was talking on the phone (in English of course) with a politically active, French-speaking business acquaintance in Montreal. We touched on the great Canadian issue of the day, and I foolishly got into apologizing for my own inability to speak French properly, despite various haphazard efforts to learn.

Unlike Pierre Elliott Trudeau, my Montreal francophone acquaintance strongly supported the recognition of Quebec as a distinct society in the Meech Lake Accord. He politely brushed aside my apologies for not speaking Canada's other official language. Outside Quebec it was, he knew, difficult to find people to "practise on," and so forth. And besides, he said quite pointedly, "we don't want you to speak French."

I said that I could see how this fit with the distinct society and whatnot, but that I still felt some residual attraction to Pierre Trudeau's sense of Canadian unity. My Montreal acquaintance replied: "O Trudeau, he still wants to roll back the conquest, and I don't think anyone can really do that."

Now, a number of years later again – in the wake of the October 1995 sovereignty referendum in Quebec – it does seem to me that what used to be called "the British Conquest of Canada" in my part of the country (or simply "la conquête" in French Canada) is still the most crucial background to the increasingly tedious French and English issue in Canada today.

The ultimate futility of mere goodwill

One characteristically Canadian irony in all this is that the rest of the country has now banished the very term "British conquest" or even just "conquest" from its public vocabulary – partly out of deference to francophone Quebec. But what my French-speaking business acquaintance from Montreal was saying, I think, is that, no matter how many historic turns of phrase we may banish, la conquête did happen. And it has had consequences that we cannot escape, even in the age of high technology.

Madeleine's husband, the historian Walt, points out that by trying to forget the conquest, we in the rest of the country have at least managed to get some distance beyond the old French and English racial or cultural antagonism that did blemish the surface of Canada in an earlier era. Even at the most obscure margins of Canadian public life today, no one says that French Canadians are a conquered people and should just get used to it.

When I was younger, I thought that archaic cultural antagonism of this sort probably was at the bottom of the French and English malaise in Canada, and that it could be overcome if there was just enough goodwill in all parts of the country. Lately, I've begun to suspect that the conquest in the middle of the eighteenth century has left another kind of legacy. And it is still creating problems that mere goodwill cannot touch.

When you strip away the small subtleties of Canadian history (including the muzzled debates on French language rights outside Quebec during the early history of the 1867 confederation), you can see it *was* the British Conquest which determined that the *majority* of people in Canada today, in both the rest of the country and the country at large, speak English. And it is because migrants from France had set down such deep roots in one part of Canada's present vast geography, *before* la conquête, that the *majority* of people in Quebec still speak French.

Democracy, of course, is about more than the will of the majority. All manner of minority rights, and many other subtle things, are very important. But the will of the majority is a crucial element in any workable democratic political system. You cannot do away with it without doing away with democracy itself.

Quite apart from race or culture or anything of that sort, "the tradition of all the dead generations" (to quote a great historical thinker, whom Walt still secretly admires) has determined that there are *two linguistic majorities* in Canada today. And the October 1995 referendum in Quebec, it seems to me, does suggest, almost clearly at last, that this probably does create an unavoidable *democratic* political problem, which neither Pierre Trudeau's nor any other extant conception of Canadian federalism can finally resolve. (And personally, I don't see anything in the 1997 federal election, or any subsequent polling data or Quebec by-elections, that alters this picture in any essential way.)

Is French a doomed language?

In fact, I can see only one straw in the prevailing wind that holds out any major prospect of getting around this problem, without some rather deep, longer-term change in our present Canadian political arrangements. The message inside the straw is that the problem doesn't ultimately matter, because the language of the French-speaking majority in Quebec is dying, anyway.

My own suspicion is that this message draws on the current confusion about "globalization." What's meant by globalization here is, in some respects, just a high technological revival of the old anglo-American imperialism, that led to la conquête in Canada in the first place. And to assert that the language of the francophone majority in Quebec is dying is just a new way of saying that French Canadians *are* a conquered people after all.

In any case, the most strident performance of such harsh music that I have recently stumbled across argues that "a unique francophone state" in Quebec is a false hope at best, because "French, like Welsh, is a doomed language. A few people may always speak it, but, within a generation, the world will mostly speak English, Mandarin, and Spanish."[*]

---

[*]Diane Francis, *Underground Nation: The Secret Economy and the Future of Canada* (Toronto: Key Porter Books, 1994), 94.

I've been running this proposition by various people I know in the rest of the country lately. It seems that you either buy it or you don't. And I just don't buy it myself.

According to some quick and dirty statistics that Ted provided me with a while ago, there are now something in the order of 124 million people in the world at large who speak French, and some 470 million who speak English.

I do recall reading in the papers recently that there is concern about the increasing international use of English in many places. Yet I still have more than a little trouble seeing how a language currently spoken by 124 million people is going to become "like Welsh ... a doomed language ... within a generation."

A nightmare on the brain of the living

A still more fundamental problem, it seems to me, is that the same kind of global thinking which suggests that French is a doomed language is also going to suggest that Canada, in either French or English, is a doomed country too.

A global future that has no room for the French language (or, for that matter, presumably for Russian, Arabic, Bengali, Japanese, German, Korean, and on and on as well) is not going to have any room for a Canada with fewer people than the golden state of California, no matter how vast and wild and romantic its geography may be. If this actually is what fate has in store for the universe, there is absolutely no point in worrying about what will happen to Canada (or Quebec) at all.

In fact, I think it's only from the first-class cabin of an airplane that a future where "the world will mostly speak English, Mandarin, and Spanish," within a generation, can look remotely plausible. The vast majority of us everywhere do not travel first class in airplanes. And this is just one reason why what really happens in history is constantly surprising people who do.

Meanwhile, back in northern North America, Ted says the only practical working assumption is that for as long as there is a Canada, there is also going to be a French-speaking majority in Quebec. Whatever else he may or may not be right or wrong about, I'm as certain as I can be that he's right about this.

As strange as it may seem when the television set is blaring, neither Quebec nor the rest of Canada today can finally escape la conquête – even though it happened as long ago as the middle of the eighteenth century. (Or, as Abraham Lincoln remarked on the eve of the American Civil War in the middle of the nineteenth century, even in the new world, "we cannot escape history.") In at least one respect, Veronica is probably right as well: if we are going to have any future ourselves, we, in the rest of Canada, just aren't going to be able to escape the francophone majority in Quebec in the twenty-first century either.

Here, as elsewhere, the "tradition of all the dead generations" – to complete the thought of the great historical thinker, whom Walt still secretly admires – "weighs like a nightmare on the brain of the living." And every time I wake up from this nightmare myself, my own case of confusion about the future of Canada and Quebec seems even more impossible than it did before.

Exhibit 10
The World's Fifteen
Most Widely Spoken Languages, 1993

(Millions of Speakers Worldwide)

Mandarin (China)	952
English	**470**
Hindi (India)	418
Spanish	381
Russian	288
Arabic	219
Bengali (India)	196
Portuguese	182
Malay-Indonesian	155
Japanese	126
French	**124**
German	121
Urdu (Pakistan, India)	100
Punjabi (India, Pakistan)	94
Korean	75

SOURCE: S. Culbert, University of Washington, Seattle.

Three

WHY THE LOYALISTS WERE WRONG AND THE FUR TRADERS WERE RIGHT

8

After the Fall

It would be a mistake to dwell too long on Pierre Trudeau's contribution to our current Canadian confusion. Ted says that "his failures are instructive but hardly definitive." (And if Canada does survive, "we may come to give Trudeau's achievements beyond the language issue much more credit than we do now.")

Besides, when your confusion becomes deeply impossible, it's a sign that blaming other people is not going to work. In this case your only ultimate option is some more intense self-examination. My own feeling is that we in the rest of the country have reached a point where we could benefit from applying some tough love to ourselves. And the only way out of our present impossible confusion that I can see is to start cutting some straighter path through a lot of historic confusion, about just how we have arrived at our present impossibly confused state.

The empire strikes out

One way of beginning here is to ponder a particular set of questions about our present troubles and the real Canadian past. It is often enough said, for instance, that the confederation of 1867 has now been around for well over 125 years. Throughout this period, there have been language statistics of a similar sort to the ones that are driving the current Quebec sovereigntist movement. There have been *two geographically concentrated linguistic majorities* in Canada, as we know it today, since the later nineteenth century. Why has it only been since the 1960s that this has threatened to tear Canada apart?

Put another way, the awkward Canadian circumstances of the unilingual francophone majority in Quebec didn't used to be such a big problem. The more than 80% of the population in Quebec that reports its mother tongue as French didn't used to be such a big problem either. Why are they such big problems now? What used to work that isn't working any more? And why has it just stopped working in the last few decades?

I think that many of us in the rest of the country have almost forgotten the obvious answer to all these questions. On several counts, we are now (rightly enough) embarrassed by a great deal of what we see as our quite slender past, and we have tried to forget it. In the process, we have haphazardly fallen into the sloppy habit of *pretending that Canada has for a long time been something that it has only quite recently started to become.*

In fact, the obvious great event of the 1960s that finally precipitated the not-so-long march to our current impossible confusion was the start of the almost final phases in the global decline and fall of the British empire – an event which had begun in earnest between the two world wars. I put this to Veronica over the phone a while ago, and her reaction was: "For God's sake, the last thing we need to start talking about right now is the British empire." But I think she is wrong. The great dismantling of the old "Empire and Commonwealth" in the 1960s is where the troubles of Canada and Quebec in the 1990s really begin.

The fall of the old dominion

Put another way again, the Canada that began on July 1, 1867, as the first modern political expression of the geographic unity which had arisen during the previous three centuries, was (as the founder of what now calls itself "Canada's national newspaper" took pains to stress many years ago now) **"not a nation."** It was just the first self-governing dominion of the British empire.

The British Dominion of Canada was more than a mere colony of what Walt only somewhat sarcastically calls "the greatest empire since Rome." But it was less than a real country as well. And, as Walt also likes to say, "None of the fathers of the 1867 confederation would have imagined that what they fathered was anything quite like a democracy."

In this same spirit, if the Dominion of Canada still existed today, it actually could be said that it did have a history which stretches back for more than 125 years. Yet, though there are still

---

The Globe, October 17, 1874. And see P.B. Waite, *Canada 1874–1896: Arduous Destiny* (Toronto: McClelland and Stewart, 1971), 34–37.

a few among us who refuse to hear the good news, the Dominion of Canada has, in fact, almost altogether disappeared.

Well within the lifetimes of many among us now, the old dominion has been superseded by what Ted calls "an aspiring democratic national state." Walt says that the history of Canada in this sense stretches back for mere decades, at most. And "throughout this period the legitimacy of the Canadian democratic national state has been persistently challenged by the sovereigntist movement in Quebec."

The new democracy that had to arise, at last

Of course, for the moment the "Queen of Canada" is still said to be our head of state. Canada still belongs to a vague international organization known as the Commonwealth of Nations. And some present-day malcontents at Canada's national newspaper have lately been conducting a futile campaign to have the name of the official birthday of the aspiring democratic national state (Canada Day) changed back to its original name of Dominion Day.

The practical point here, however, is that the *real* Dominion of Canada was symbiotically dependent on the real British empire, to resolve some of the dominion's more fundamental domestic problems. One of these problems was the looming and pervasive influence of a more and more muscular USA. Another was the French Canadian fact.

When the British empire finally became almost altogether obsolete in the 1960s, so did its dependent self-governing British Dominion of Canada. The fundamental domestic problems that the old empire had helped the old dominion resolve took out new leases on life. And Canada especially began to face new pressures from the francophone majority in Quebec. (So long as Canada wasn't a national democracy in its own right, the francophone majority in Quebec could evade the prospect of being ruled forever by the anglophone majority in Canada at large. But once an aspiring Canadian democracy did begin to take its own distinctive shape, Quebec was bound to explode in protest.)

Historians like Walt will tell you that, in a few respects, Canada had started to become a national democracy as early as the early twentieth century. Yet, as Walt himself points out, it "moved very slowly and hesitantly in this direction, because its leadership had a finely tuned sense of just how much the local dominion depended on the global empire, to keep the potent forces of both American and French Canadian nationalism at bay." It wasn't until the empire itself began to vanish forever, in the 1960s, that Canada *had* to become an altogether real democracy at last – whether it wanted to or not.

Exhibit 11
Ethnic Origin
Canada, 1901–1961

Group	% Population in Group			
	1901	1921	1941	1961
Aboriginal	2.4	1.3	1.4	1.2
British	**57.0**	**55.4**	**49.7**	**43.8**
French	30.7	27.8	30.2	30.4
Other European	8.6	14.2	17.8	22.6
Asian	0.4	0.8	0.6	0.7
Other	0.9	0.5	0.3	1.3
All Origins	**100.0**	**100.0**	**100.0**	**100.0**

SOURCE: Statistics Canada.

9

Old Loyalist Mythologies

For as long as I can remember, my brother and sister and I, despite all our other differences, have been warm supporters of the disappearance of the old British Dominion of Canada, and its replacement by the aspiring Canadian democracy of today. But I also like to think that I can appreciate certain now-vanished virtues of the way things used to be.

Walt says that even though the Dominion of Canada was "a transitional political enterprise, built on assumptions which its more thoughtful inhabitants always knew were false," it did have some things which today's aspiring national democracy still lacks. And one of them was a deceptively simple answer to the endless nagging question: "What is Canada all about, anyway?"

Madeleine's blue dress

Walt improved my understanding of the deep background to this deceptively simple answer a number of years ago now, during a congenial long dinner at his and Madeleine's house (in the exurbs of the national capital region, on the banks of the Ottawa River). I particularly remember the occasion because Madeleine was wearing a stunning blue summer dress, which went almost all the way down to her waist at the back.

According to what Walt called the old loyalist theory, "modern Canada" did formally trace its origins back to the northern North American "conquest," which took place during the global Seven Years' War of 1756–1763. (And thus the words of the old British Canadian anthem, effectively proscribed in the more recent democratic national past, began: "In days of yore, from Britain's shore, Wolfe the conquering hero bore.")[*]

The conquest in this sense, however, was just an initial foray

---

[*]For Madeleine's benefit, I recalled the alternate words to the anthem learned on the street in the 1950s, when I was in elementary school. They began: "In days of yore, before the war," and ended with "and babies were prevented."

into the promised northern wilderness, staking out fresh ground for chosen people who were not quite ready to come. The actual origins of English-speaking Canada only stretched back to the subsequent American Revolution or War of Independence, from 1776 to 1783. At the end of this conflict "some 50,000" so-called "United Empire Loyalist" refugees (perhaps a still rather generous present-day estimate, Walt says) moved north, into several parts of the remaining British North American territory, in what is now eastern and central Canada.

In fact these people were quite a mixed lot. But they would be more selectively remembered as American Tories, who had opposed the Patriot revolution in the old Thirteen Colonies, on grounds of political philosophy. In this same spirit, the Canada that became the British empire's first self-governing dominion in 1867 was the historic refuge of those *British* North Americans who had remained loyal to the Crown in the ill-conceived colonial revolt. The first British empire in America had embarked on the wayward experiment of the USA. Yet a transplanted fragment of the old imperial grandeur would live on in Canada, at the edge of the vast wilderness in the most northern parts of the new world.

Veronica's contribution

Of course (Walt went on to explain), one big wrinkle in this old loyalist theory was that, at the time of the actual migrations, part of the northern territory into which the English-speaking loyalist refugees moved was already occupied by rather larger numbers of French-speaking "Canadiens." They were descendants of migrants from France across the ocean, most of whom had arrived in the seventeenth century, long before la conquête.

Yet the Catholic French Canadians were heirs of the feudal traditions of France before the French Revolution of 1789. Like the British American Tory loyalists, they, too, could be plausibly portrayed as political counter-revolutionaries. And the counter-revolutionary Roman Catholic church in French-speaking Quebec would become a kind of half-captive partner to the British empire in English-speaking Canada. (At this point, my sister couldn't resist adding her own contribution. "And it's not exactly an accident," she said, "that both the Empire in the rest of the country and the Church in Quebec would finally start to disappear together, after the Second World War.")

In French-speaking Quebec today there is apparently a stronger memory of all this than there is in the rest of the country. And my own sense is that this memory has something to do with both the present-day notion of Canada as a place of two founding peoples, and the related notion of some new partnership between a sovereign French-speaking Quebec and some more or less analogous English Canada.

The big trouble with these and all similar notions, however, is that the United Empire Loyalist legend of modern Canadian origins has always had a lot more to do with political mythology than with what really happened in history. Ted, who was born and raised in Calgary, had stressed this point over dessert during the dinner at Walt and Madeleine's. I and everyone else there that evening had warmly agreed (though my memory here is somewhat confused by an image of Madeleine's near-naked back, as she went around the table pouring coffee, after dessert).

Ted's critique

Urged on by Ted, Walt helped us compile a list of just the most obvious cases where the old loyalist mythologies depart quite dramatically from the unvarnished truth. To start with, in both the ancient Atlantic fisheries and the inland fur-trade adventures of the Hudson's Bay Company, there was already an English-speaking presence in what is now Canada, well over 100 years before the coming of the loyalists in the late eighteenth century.

Similarly, anglo-American frontier migrants from what subsequently became the USA had begun to settle in what is now Nova Scotia a generation before the American War of Independence. The loyalist migrations of the 1780s themselves were only one incident in a much longer and deeper history of northwesterly *American* frontier migration into the present Canadian territory.

Demographically, the new "loyalist province" of New Brunswick (also the only present province outside Quebec with a comparatively large francophone minority) was the only part of

Canada today where the loyalist migrations made a decisive numerical contribution to the early English-speaking population.

Canada's present most-populous province of Ontario adopted a fanciful loyalist motto in the early twentieth century. But the great majority of new settlers there before the War of 1812 were politically neutral frontier migrants – the same sorts of people who would later move into the Mexican province of Texas.* From the standpoint of demographic weight, again, the real *British* population in nineteenth-century Ontario arrived directly from the United Kingdom between 1820 and 1860.

The early Red River settlement in what subsequently became Manitoba was essentially a retirement community for the culturally diverse employees of the Canadian fur trade. The "last best west" in anglo North America, in what are now the three prairie provinces of Canada, attracted yet another wave of American frontier migrants during the later nineteenth and earlier twentieth centuries. But by this point, both the United Empire Loyalists and the War of Independence were ancient history.

Once again, the people who finally contributed to what there was of a British population in the prairie provinces, and especially British Columbia, came directly from the United Kingdom, long after the revolution in the USA. (Some three-quarters of the population in the crown colony of British Columbia, Ted pointed out, was still made up of North American aboriginal peoples when BC joined the new Dominion of Canada in 1871.)

Riding on the highway

In the car, on the way back from Walt and Madeleine's that evening, I summarized my own views on the larger subject for the benefit of my wife. Several times she begged me to be quiet and just enjoy the summer night air. But I persisted because I knew that, deep down, she felt a need for some summary of this sort.

In fact, I went on, the weaknesses of the United Empire

---

*And Walt says that those who doubt this point should consult the "standard text" – Gerald M. Craig, *Upper Canada: The Formative Years, 1784–1841* (Toronto: McClelland and Stewart, 1963), 43–49.

Loyalist legend as an account of what really happened in history, even after la conquête, are so palpable as to make it quite unlikely that anyone ever took it all that seriously in this regard.

At most, only an extremely small fraction of the present English-speaking Canadian population can trace its ancestry back to the loyalist migrations. And at their worst, the various loyalist mythologies that haunted the Dominion of Canada were rickety vehicles of social snobbery and political exclusion, which large numbers of the dominion's inhabitants simply ignored.

This raises the slightly puzzling question of why some otherwise highly intelligent people (the late novelist Robertson Davies is an example that immediately jumps to mind) have been prepared to invoke the loyalist legend with some apparent enthusiasm, even in the comparatively recent past.

The best answer I can come up with, I told my wife, was that for several generations the legend did provide a deceptively simple answer to the recurrent gnawing question of what Canada is all about. And it did this in a way which offered a historically inaccurate, but still somewhat poetic, explanation of two real facts of Canadian life that remained more or less intact down to some point not too long after the Second World War.

The first of these facts involved more than a century and a quarter of mass migrations from the United Kingdom, especially to the central and far western parts of present-day Canada. The second was the dominion's continuing symbiotic and frequently enthusiastic relationship with the political, economic, and cultural institutions of the British empire. (It was of course never true, as the Hollywood movie industry once seemed to imagine, that English-speaking Canadians born in Canada spoke with British accents, but that is another matter.)

My wife's last word

The increasingly diverse migrations that have come to shape the Canadian population in the twentieth century, of course (inside and outside, but especially outside Quebec), have only added to the burden of the loyalist theory's historical inaccuracy, even in this last sense. Down to the Second World War at least a bare majority of Canada's more recent inhabitants were of British descent – even if the ancestors of most of the people involved had come directly from the United Kingdom, rather than the ancient British Thirteen Colonies in America. Yet by as early as the 1950s, another bare majority of people in the country at large (including Quebec) were *not* of British descent. By the early 1990s even the majority of people in the rest of the country, or Canada outside Quebec, were not of British descent either.

Even here there are still some residual imperial echoes. Many recent migrants to Canada, while not exactly of British descent, are, nonetheless, from parts of the world that also used to be mixed up with the British empire – in India or Pakistan or Hong Kong or Singapore or Malaysia or Somalia or Nigeria or Jamaica or Trinidad and Tobago, and on and on.

In my own advancing age, I have come to appreciate that these and certain other continuing residues of Canada's British imperial past still have some progressive attractions. And I am somewhat less inclined than I used to be to mock *all* the old loyalist mythologies. It still does seem to me, however, that loyalism was an essentially anti-democratic force, that kept Canada in a kind of political and cultural nursery for far too long.

And (my wife added, in an at last successful bid to calm me down, as we rode through the Ottawa exurbs, back to our hotel downtown): "Whatever you might think about such things, the simplest truth is that the notion of even an unreal country built on historic loyalty to a grand global empire, no longer makes even poetic sense, once the empire itself has disappeared."

Exhibit 12
Immigrant Population
Canada and Provinces and Territories, 1991
As percentage of total population

Province/Territory	Immigrant Population* %
Ontario	23.8
British Columbia	22.3
Alberta	15.1
Manitoba	12.8
Yukon	10.7
Quebec	**8.7**
Saskatchewan	5.9
Northwest Territories	4.9
Nova Scotia	4.4
New Brunswick	3.4
Prince Edward Island	3.2
Newfoundland	1.5
Rest of Canada	**18.6**
CANADA	16.1

*Permanent residents of Canada born outside Canada.

SOURCE: Statistics Canada.

10

New Legends of the Fur Trade

Walt says that if the loyalist theory of modern Canadian origins were the only such theory to have put down roots during the past two centuries of English-speaking Canadian history, then the annexation of large parts of Canada today by the USA would probably be close to a historical certainty – with only the exact form and related sundry details left for the future to decide.

Yet, as fate would have it, the loyal participation of Canadian troops in the forces of the British empire during the First World War marked a minor watershed in the cautious early growth of popular national democratic sentiment in English-speaking Canada. The period between the two world wars was also a time when thoughtful people in various places began to understand that the British empire would not last forever. And another more native view of what Canada is all about gradually arose from a subterranean local ferment, in the 1920s, 1930s, and 1940s.

Adventures in the academic wilderness

As Walt tells the story, in the 1920s several handfuls of young men, who had discovered nascent Canadian national feelings on the battlefields of Europe, between 1914 and 1918, took up positions in the Dominion of Canada's fledgling English-language system of higher education. And they began to wonder what would happen to Canada when the British empire did finally end.

As an aid to their wondering, they started to look at what had really taken place in northern North America, from the early European contacts with aboriginal peoples in the late fifteenth and sixteenth centuries down to the present.* By the 1930s, they had begun to piece together a fresh account of the growth of Canada's geographic unity, sparked by diverse assortments of

---

*In fact, the earliest European contacts with the most northerly parts of the new world involve various Norse voyages of the late tenth and early eleventh centuries. But they did not last, or lead to enduring later developments.

European and aboriginal and other peoples, and the aboriginal transportation technology of the canoe and portage.

The somewhat grudgingly acknowledged great guru in this enterprise was the angular economist Harold Innis, whose 1930 book on *The Fur Trade in Canada* still stands as a classic introduction to what Walt likes to call the "post-modern fur trade legend of what Canada is *really* all about." Walt argues that this legend probably has a lot to do with whatever prospects there are for an independent Canadian future, regardless of what may or may not happen in the next referendum that may or may not take place in Quebec. And, as strange and even crazy as this may seem to be at first, I have lately begun to think that he is probably right.

Ironically enough, like Lucien Bouchard in a later era, Harold Innis married an attractive girl from the United States. He also became what a recent book has characterized as "the first and last non-American" to be elected president of the American Economic Association. It may or may not be to his credit as well, Walt says, that his cryptic writing of the 1940s on *Empire and Communications* helped inspire Marshall McLuhan's cryptic utterances of the 1960s, on the future of the global village. In the end, as the *Times Literary Supplement* in the United Kingdom once somewhat sarcastically explained, Harold Innis was "Canada's first and perhaps only genuine intellectual."

The last ice sheets

According to Walt (again), at least one version of the fur trade legend acquired an early Canadian history text of sorts, when Harold Innis's friend Arthur Lower published a book with the somewhat premature title, *Colony to Nation*, in 1946. A few years later, Innis noted the new "American imperialism" that was replacing the old "British imperialism," in the wake of the Second World War. And he quipped that Canada's ultimate story looked a lot more like "colony to nation to colony."

The increasing Americanization of the English-speaking Canadian university scene in the last half of the twentieth century, Walt says, has pushed the continuing development of the Canadian fur trade legend away from the centre of current academic life, in virtually all parts of the country. The legend's more recent growth has tended to take place in what Innis himself predicted would become "a Canadian underground."

A volume in its own right could nonetheless be written on additions to the relevant "literature," since the somewhat premature death of Harold Innis in 1952. On Walt's advice, I would just pick two comparatively recent additions to my own bookshelves, as illustrations of the current state of the art.

The first is Sylvia Van Kirk's *Many Tender Ties: Women in Fur Trade Society, 1670–1870*. First published in 1980, it is one of several books that have begun to redress an essentially false *machismo* in some earlier accounts of the fur trade legend

The book that probably still gives the best general account of at least the comparatively recent state of the art is the first volume of the new *Historical Atlas of Canada*, which bears the subtitle *From the Beginnings to 1800*. Published in 1987, it is edited by the geographer R. Cole Harris, with cartography directed by Geoffrey Matthews. The plates in the volume appropriately begin with "The Last Ice Sheets, 18,000–10,000 B.C." And one current short answer to the question, "What is Canada," the map here suggests, is that it's the part of North America entirely covered by ice in 18,000 BC.

Equally appropriately, the volume ends with a plate called "Native Canada, ca. 1820." And this is reminiscent of one of the most striking passages in the conclusion to Harold Innis's pioneering book of 1930: "'The lords of the lakes and forest have passed away' but their work will endure in the boundaries of the Dominion of Canada and in Canadian institutional life ... We have not yet realized that the Indian and his culture were fundamental to the growth of Canadian institutions."

The real masters of the country

The fur trade legend in Canada today is not as easy to summarize in a short space as the earlier loyalist mythologies. Innis's classic account fills up an often dense and hard-to-read book of some four hundred pages. The legend is deep and complex, Walt argues, because it is about the deep and complex lives of many different kinds of people, over very long periods of time.

Walt also suggests that "you probably have to allow for some initial willing suspension of disbelief if you want to grasp what the fur trade legend is ultimately all about." And this has certainly been my own experience (though my wife says that she thinks this is just Walt's way of keeping the story mysterious).

In the first place the legend is simply about how the expansion of the "Indian and European" fur trade in northern North America, from the sixteenth to the earlier nineteenth centuries, created the geographic unity of Canada as we know it today, and laid the foundations for what Harold Innis called "Canadian institutional life." But the legend's most resounding depths involve a lot more than this.

Madeleine, who has a spiritual side, once said that, for her, the fur trade legend her husband talks so much about has nothing to do with reading books. It is something you apprehend around a fire – or from the end of a dock, or somewhere at the water's edge – "up north," if you "look at the midnight sky and are lucky enough to see the northern lights."

In the very end, the fur trade legend is probably more a way of thinking about the future than a story about the past. It is not telling you what to think. It is just offering information about what has already happened, and pointing to some related, open-ended directions. You have to make up your own mind.

The seventeenth-century Jesuits from France, according to the McGill University anthropologist Bruce Trigger, "described dreams as being the principal god" of the aboriginal people in Canada and "the 'real masters of the country.'" And because "dreams predicted future events and could warn people of the dangers that threatened them, the advice of dreams might be followed in preference to that of leading chiefs." Walt once told me that he sometimes thought Madeleine was right in a way, and that the fur trade legend finally was a kind of collective dream of this sort, that most of us were still only beginning to understand.

Exhibit 13
Immigrant Population
Census Metropolitan Areas, 1991
As percentage of total population

Ten largest CMAs in bold type

Immigrant Population %		Immigrant Population %	
Toronto, Ont	**38.0**	Regina, Sask	8.4
Vancouver, BC	**30.1**	Saskatoon, Sask	8.2
Hamilton, Ont	**23.5**	Sudbury, Ont	8.2
Kitchener, Ont	21.5	Halifax, NS	6.5
Windsor, Ont	20.8	Saint John, NB	4.3
Calgary, Alta	**20.3**	Sherbrooke, Que	3.8
Victoria, BC	19.5	St. John's, Nfld	2.8
St. Catharines, Ont	18.9	**Québec, Que**	**2.2**
London, Ont	**18.8**	Trois-Rivières, Que	1.3
Edmonton, Alta	**18.4**	Chicoutimi, Que	0.7
Winnipeg, Man	**17.5**		
Oshawa, Ont	17.2		
Montréal, Que	**16.8**	QUEBEC	8.7
Ottawa-Hull	**14.8**	CANADA	16.1
Thunder Bay, Ont	13.2	REST OF CANADA	18.6

SOURCE: Statistics Canada.

11

Early Underground Adventures*

It helps to dispel my own current impossible confusion to say that just as the earlier loyalist mythologies served as a kind of implicit philosophy for the old Dominion of Canada, the new legend of the fur trade at least ought to be playing a similar role for today's aspiring Canadian democracy, which began to replace the old dominion at some point after the Second World War.

In fact, Walt, the fur trade historian, argues that something of this sort actually did start to happen, during the long federal regime of Pierre Trudeau, from 1968 to 1984. As I've noted earlier, Trudeau wrote a foreword to his paddling colleague Eric Morse's short book of 1969 on *Fur Trade Canoe Routes of Canada: Then and Now*. And not long ago, my wife received a related package from Madeleine in the mail. It included a copy of a recent article from an archaeological journal, in which Walt had marked a salient passage with a yellow felt pen:

> [D]espite considerable early research into the fur trade period conducted by historians in the 1930s and 1940s, little systematic or intensive archaeological excavations of fur trade posts occurred until the 1960s, most of which was sponsored by the Canadian Historic Sites Service (later Parks Canada) and various universities in the western provinces ... This fur trade research in the 1960s and 1970s, and its focus on culture and history, actually reflected the political agenda of the federal government in its attempt to define, through the restoration and reconstruction of fur trade posts, a national identity for Canada.*

The culture of the fur trade

As Walt observed in a scribbled note, this kind of activity also "reflects the limitations of the bureaucratic imagination." It flows

---

*The article Walt sent is by a Jane H. Kelley and Ronald F. Williamson. It appeared in the January 1996 issue of *American Antiquity*.

from a superficial grasp of the deeper fur trade legend, at best. And, inspired by a related earlier conversation with Walt, I think something similar happened, when one of the fur trade legend's particular themes found expression in the rather bloodless multiculturalism policy adopted by the Trudeau regime in 1971.

Harold Innis's classic book of 1930 bore the subtitle, *An Introduction to Canadian Economic History*, and the inter-war generation had concentrated on the economic development aspects of the fur trade legend. Innis himself, however, was deeply intrigued by culture, in virtually all the senses of this multidimensional term. The new legend of Canadian origins that his book of 1930 did so much to crystallize has, when you start to think about it, some obvious enough cultural implications.

I don't know just how Pierre Trudeau's grasp of these implications relates to the English-speaking Canadian academic writing of Innis and his colleagues between the two world wars. Like Madeleine, I think the legend is authentic in the sense that you do not need to have read any particular books to acquire some vital intimation of just what it means.

Trudeau, on the other hand, does read books. The essays he wrote before he became prime minister suggest that, unlike many francophone intellectuals in Quebec, he did have some acquaintance with the writing of anglophone intellectuals in the rest of Canada (genuine or otherwise). But Walt says that Trudeau's grasp of the fur trade legend also has a lot to do with his own explorations of the Canadian past, in and out of canoes.

The long history of Canadian diversity

Wherever Trudeau's ideas came from, the crucial point about multiculturalism is that, according to the fur trade legend, Canada has a *long founding era*, from the sixteenth to the nineteenth centuries. But the spread of the Indian and European fur trade, along the inland waterways from the Atlantic, to the Arctic, to the Pacific oceans, was the work of a vast assortment of human beings. And Canada does *not* really *have any founding peoples*.

Both the transportation technology of the canoe and portage, and several major varieties of the Indian and his culture, played key roles in the founding of Canada in this sense. So did several major varieties of Europeans – especially French and English (including Irish, many Scots, Welsh, and stalwart Orkney Islanders employed by the Hudson's Bay Company), but others as well: Dutch, German, Swiss, Catholic, Jewish, Protestant, and even several varieties of anglo-American.

The primary sources of Canadian fur trade history make clear that some people of African and even, it seems, Asian descent were involved in Canada's long founding era as well.[*] Walt says that there are even early nineteenth-century references to a party of Hawaiians, at the North West Company's (recently restored) inland headquarters in the present Canadian city of Thunder Bay.

My own guess is that somehow Trudeau did appreciate this exotic cultural diversity in the deepest Canadian past. And he had an imaginative grasp of the role it could play in the future of the aspiring new democracy of the late twentieth century and beyond. Alas, the thin and artificial multicultural policy that he inspired the federal bureaucracy in Ottawa to create makes almost no one happy today. But I don't think this is exactly Trudeau's fault. The key trouble is that the collective dream of the fur trade legend is still not deep and wide enough to mobilize the full potential of our remarkable heritage in northern North America. And for this, no doubt, all of us in Canada (non-immigrant and immigrant alike) have no one to blame but ourselves.

The language of the fur trade

My sister, Veronica, thinks it's just "romanticizing the past" to "talk too much about the heritage of the fur trade in Canada." (She once told me in private that "Walt is a wonderful guy, but both he and Madeleine don't exactly live in the real world.") Yet Veronica also likes to argue that if you *are* going to talk this way, you ought to recognize that the fur trade legend of Canada's real origins "also implies Pierre Trudeau's particular kind of French

---

[*]On the conventional academic view today, the aboriginal peoples of the new world are of Asian descent as well, though many current Canadian aboriginal leaders are sceptical about this view, at best.

and English bilingual vision of the Canadian future."

Walt's own view here is that the legend explains how the northern North American geographic unity created by the expansion of the Indian and European fur trade was brought into an emerging world economy, through the rival sea-borne empires of France and Britain. For better or worse, European imperialism in this sense has everywhere bequeathed the dominant languages spoken in the new world today. And, historically, the languages bequeathed to Canada certainly are English *and French*.

Yet, Walt's argument is that while this is not inconsistent with Trudeau's bilingual vision, the vision itself does not really flow from the fur trade legend. Trudeau's case about language has more to do with the democratization of the geographic fact bequeathed by the fur trade, and the distribution of anglophones and francophones, in the middle of the twentieth century.

If French-speaking Quebec had not been so tenacious, Walt says, the linguistic logic of the fur trade heritage might flow in other directions. English did eventually become the, as it were, official language of both the Hudson's Bay and North West companies – the two great private-sector economic institutions which finally brought the fur trade in Canada into its golden age, during the early nineteenth century. If you look strictly at the *transcontinental* trade down to the early 1820s, Walt says, you could even argue that if the French language has some historic special status in Canada, Cree and perhaps a few other aboriginal languages ought to have some similar special status, as well.

Rising to the heights of national occasions

Veronica's own lifetime companion, Ted, once told me a related tale about Harold Innis's friend, Arthur Lower. The "soul" of Canada, Lower apparently wrote in the final pages of his prematurely entitled 1946 history textbook, *Colony to Nation,* is ultimately in the geography of "the northern wildernesses ... not in the English language or the French."

But the same pages also have some harsh things to say about the leadership of the old Dominion of Canada. And Ted feels Lower's remarks here inadvertently cast light on the true stature of Pierre Elliott Trudeau, who first brought some authentic appreciation of the fur trade legend to Canadian public life.

The largely English-speaking Canadian political leaders of his own day, Lower argued in 1946, had "their good points ... No group of men could frame a better set of exchange regulations." But they were "singularly lacking" in "creative imagination," and "they could not rise to the height of a national occasion." As Ted has put it, "Whatever else you say, Trudeau could rise to the height of a national occasion, and he did, several times."

My own related view is that while Trudeau's language policy has almost certainly failed, his passion for Canada's geographic fact remains an inspiration. (And, if there is such a thing as "a real Canadian," it probably looks quite a lot like him.)

Exhibit 14
Ethnic Origin
Rest of Canada and Quebec, 1991

REST OF CANADA		QUEBEC	
% Population in Group		% Population in Group	
Multiple origins	35.8	**French origins**	**74.5**
British origins	**26.4**	Multiple origins	8.4
European origins	18.1	European origins	7.2
Asian and African origins	7.1	**British origins**	**4.2**
French origins	**5.3**	Asian and African origins	3.0
Aboriginal origins	**2.0**	**Aboriginal origins**	**1.0**
All Other origins	5.3	All Other origins	1.7

SOURCE: Statistics Canada.

Four

THE MAPLE LEAF RAG
(An interlude)

12

An Almost Inaudible Revolution

You can watch almost anything on television today. On June 23, 1997, from the comfort of my small couch in the TV room upstairs, I watched the royal yacht, *Britannia*, cruise majestically into the crowded harbour at Hong Kong, for one last time. The ship and her crew were ending a long journey that had begun in January at Malta on the Mediterranean Sea.

In another, deeper sense (I thought, working my way through a bag of nachos), they were ending a much longer journey that had begun some fifty years before – when Lord Louis Mountbatten handed over the British Raj on the Indian subcontinent to the successor states of India and Pakistan, on August 15, 1947.

The end of the British Raj in India in 1947 had marked the beginning of the end of the wider British empire. The transfer of the British crown colony of Hong Kong to the Peoples' Republic of China in 1997 is probably as close as we are going to get to some final sign that the British empire has now, almost utterly and absolutely, ended forever.

Up here in the obscure attic of North America, we can also say that between these same two dates, the old Dominion of Canada rather haphazardly evolved into the aspiring Canadian democratic national state we know today. And if the evolution is still incomplete, we long ago passed the point of no return.

The first Citizenship Act in 1947

Pierre Trudeau's first fur-trade-legend regime at Ottawa, from 1968 to 1984, marked an accelerated phase in this process. And it *is* clear enough now that certain key directions in which Trudeau tried to point the new democracy are not going to work. (At least it's clear enough to me – and even to people like my sister who, whatever else she might say, did finally vote Yes in the 1992 referendum on the Charlottetown Accord.)

As we wonder about exactly what Trudeau's particular failures might mean for the future, however, I think it helps to remember that he did not actually start the new democracy himself. The creation of the aspiring national state wasn't just a reaction to the sovereigntist movement in Quebec, either. As reluctant as some parts of it sometimes seemed to be (still nostalgic for the grandeur of the empire on which the sun never set), the "rest of the country" played crucial roles of its own.

In fact, Ted argues that in the late 1960s Trudeau was almost deliberately handed a kind of erector set for the new democracy. It had been packaged during the previous two decades – by the same grey anglophones with "good points," who could frame excellent sets of exchange regulations, but did not know how to rise to the heights of national occasions, themselves.

Whatever the deepest truth may be, the first bold step along the path of no return did take place just as the British Raj in India was coming to an end in 1947. According to the 1988 or "120th Anniversary edition" of the *Canada Year Book* (which my wife, with a touch of sarcasm, I think, bought for me as a gift), the "Canadian Citizenship Act, passed in 1947," was "the first independent naturalization law to be enacted in the Commonwealth" and "created the status of a Canadian citizen as distinct from that of a British subject."

I was surprised myself when I stumbled across this entry in the *Canada Year Book* – while watching something about the Meech Lake Accord on TV. I confirmed the point over the phone with Walt. He says that many Canadians today think "the status of a Canadian citizen" was established in 1867. But it wasn't. Until 1947 residents of Canada were merely "British subjects."[*]

In any case, a democracy has citizens not subjects. And when the parliament of Canada passed the Citizenship Act of 1947, it haphazardly set off in some new democratic directions.

---

[*]Walt reports that there are two additional wrinkles here. First, an act passed in 1921, in the wake of the First World War, had already given Canadians travelling abroad "the right to call themselves 'Canadian Nationals,'" thus distinguishing them from other British subjects." And second, even after 1947 Canadian citizens continued to qualify as British subjects, until the Trudeau regime's new Citizenship Act, which took effect in 1977.

Ending the last legal ties that bound us

There were a number of other developments in the more or less immediate wake of the Second World War that pointed in similar new directions. But just contemplating even a short list reminds me of how much more interesting the trees seemed, outside the windows of some chalk-dusted classroom of my youth. No matter how you present it, the evolution of political nationality in Canada is a tedious subject, and that may be the best explanation of why most of us know so little about it.

In 1949, for instance, the Supreme Court of Canada became the final court of appeal in the Canadian legal system, taking over this role from the so-called Judicial Committee of the Privy Council in the United Kingdom.

At this point, only one related dependent Canadian connection with the UK remained. What was then still known as the British North America Act – the legal document that had, as it were, created the first modern political expression of Canada in 1867 – was still an act of the British parliament. And only the British parliament could change or amend it.

This could or even ought to have been altered in 1931, when the so-called Statute of Westminister clarified that all British dominions (by that point Canada, Australia, New Zealand, and so forth) had full autonomy from the United Kingdom. Canadian federal and provincial governments, however, could not agree on an appropriate amending formula. Despite repeated efforts to reach an agreement of this sort, the power to amend the Canadian constitution continued to rest with the parliament in the United Kingdom, until Trudeau's Constitution Act, 1982. This was agreed to by the federal government in Ottawa and all provinces *except Quebec* (and this exception leads directly, in a formal, legal sense, to our continuing constitutional crisis today) .

The 52% solution

The long-awaited arrival of the tenth province of Newfoundland was another Canadian nation-building event of 1949.

Historically, the old British fishing colony of the north

Atlantic had pondered joining the confederation of 1867, and decided to remain aloof. Then it pondered joining Canada again in the 1890s, with the same result.

For a brief period after this, Newfoundland had become a self-governing British dominion in its own right. Then the Great Depression of the 1930s pushed it into bankruptcy, and it reluctantly reverted to the status of a directly administered colony of the United Kingdom.

In the late spring and early summer of 1948, two referendums were held on the future of Newfoundland. The second managed to produce a slim 52% majority in favour of joining Canada at last. On April 1, 1949, the will of the democratic majority took official effect. Among other things, Newfoundland was the first (and still the only) province to join Canada as the result of a popular vote. And, not surprisingly, Quebec sovereigntists today argue that if "52% Yes" was enough to bring Newfoundland into the country, it should also be enough to take Quebec out.

Canada's last viscount

As yet another early sign of the gradual transition from old British dominion to new national democracy, Vincent Massey, scion of a prominent family of farm-machinery manufacturers (and brother of the Hollywood actor, Raymond Massey), became the first Canadian-born governor general of Canada in 1952.

After consulting Walt on the phone, I have studied this matter at length, in some old texts on my bookshelves. It is probably more than enough to say that by the time of certain events of the later 1920s, which led to the formal clarifications of the Statute of Westminister in 1931, the appointment of the governor general of Canada had become a matter for the king (or queen) and the *prime minister of Canada, not* of the United Kingdom.

All Canadian governor generals of the 1930s and 1940s were, nonetheless, respectable British aristocrats, born and properly bred in the United Kingdom. Vincent Massey's two immediate predecessors had been the Earl of Athlone (1940–46) and Viscount Alexander of Tunis (1946–52).

In 1952 Louis St. Laurent became the first Canadian prime

minister who dared to appoint someone to the office who was not a British aristocrat (even though it is often said that Vincent Massey wished he were, and did his best to appear as if he was).

Exhibit 15
Population Growth
Canada and Quebec, 1871–1991

Year	Population (000s)		
	Quebec	Rest of Canada	Canada
1871	**1,191**	**2,498**	**3,689**
1881	1,360	2,965	4,325
1891	1,489	3,344	4,833
1901	**1,649**	**3,722**	**5,371**
1911	2,006	5,201	7,207
1921	2,361	6,427	8,788
1931	**2,875**	**7,502**	**10,377**
1941	3,332	8,175	11,507
1951	4,056	9,953	14,009
1961	**5,259**	**12,979**	**18,238**
1971	6,028	15,540	21,568
1981	6,438	17,905	24,343
1991	**7,081**	**21,039**	**28,120**

SOURCE: Statistics Canada.

84

13

The New Flag and All That

Anyone who was living in Canada at the time will remember that the British imperial veneer of the old dominion was still quite visible in the 1950s – especially in the earlier parts of the decade.

For the coronation of Queen Elizabeth II in 1953, everyone in my elementary-school class was given a commemorative medal to take home. The roll-down maps on our classroom walls still had everything that "belonged" to the British Empire and Commonwealth in red (or more like pink, in fact). And this still included India which, even though it had become a republic in 1949, still chose to remain "inside the Commonwealth."*

There were some extremely gentle stirrings of movement in another direction. In grade five or six we had a quite terrific history textbook called *Pirates and Pathfinders*, which strikes me now as my initial introduction to at least some vague sense of the new legend of the fur trade. (I have friends today who grew up in different places than I did but also remember this book. A somewhat related children's volume of the era was *The Map Maker* – a biography of the North West Company trader and surveyor David Thompson, which I still remember borrowing from my local bookmobile.)

In the later 1950s, the recently inaugurated CBC television ran a comparatively short-lived dramatic series called "Radisson," which tried to do for young people in Canada what Davy Crockett ("king of the wild frontier") was presumed to be doing in the USA. It recounted some alleged adventures of the French-

---

*For a very brief period, between 1947 and 1949, India had actually been a self-governing "British dominion" itself. To round the broader picture out, there had been six dominions at the time of the Statute of Westminster in 1931: Australia, Canada, the Irish Free State, Newfoundland, New Zealand, and South Africa. The Irish Free State changed its name to Eire in 1937 and became a republic in 1949. South Africa became a republic "outside the Commonwealth" in 1961. With the transformation of the British Empire and Commonwealth into the present-day Commonwealth of Nations, during the 1960s and 1970s, the whole notion of "dominion status" became redundant.

Canadian fur trader who helped found the English Hudson's Bay Company in 1670. What I remember most about this now is the schoolyard mocking of the telephone poles and hydro towers, that periodically appeared in the television wilderness, where Radisson's adventures were supposed to be taking place.

You've got to be a football hero

Finally the 1960s came along. The pace of change even in Canada began to accelerate somewhat. In the summer of 1963, I went off on my trip to the Gaspé coast in Quebec and saw "FLQ" in big white letters up on the giant rock. A year or so later, in the fall of 1964, I had begun my Canadian higher education.

I played in the football band during my first year at university. It was an intellectually painless way of acquiring credits that you otherwise had to obtain by taking a course in religious knowledge. The band in those days was directed by a mature student. We were all young and on the edge of the future. From the first game of the season, when we marched out onto the field, our majorettes carried the brand new Canadian flag.

At this point, the exact design of the thing was still in motion. For our first few games, we carried a white flag with a red maple leaf in the centre and blue bars at either end. Then our director apparently heard something from Ottawa. The bars were going to be changed – for obscure heraldic reasons that no one even wanted to understand. We finished the season carrying a red maple leaf with red bars on a white background.

This flag design would not be formally proclaimed in Ottawa until February 15, 1965. By this point, the football season was over. I was playing in the much smaller hockey band, and no one in this organization was ever sober long enough to carry anything very far. But I have always enjoyed remembering that the university football band I played in was a pioneer in showing the new Canadian flag. (This is also, I think, the only event in my life that my brother and sister have both unambiguously approved. And when I told the story to Madeleine, on a cold winter night several years ago, she said that she approved too.)

A meditation on the flag

Walt says that if you had to pick a single point at which the transition from the old dominion to the new democracy in Canada really started to gain momentum, the proclamation of the new flag in 1965 is probably the one to choose.

Before this, the flags most often flown in Canada were the British Union Jack, and the so-called Canadian red ensign (a red flag with a small Union Jack in the upper left-hand corner and the Canadian coat of arms in the centre-right).* The Liberal Party of Canada had begun to promise that Canada would have a distinctive flag of its own in the early 1920s, just after the First World War. It revived the promise in the mid-1940s, at the end of the Second World War. But nothing actually happened in either case. For many complicated reasons, the old dominion *was* reluctant to leave the Union Jack behind.

So it wasn't until the mid-1960s – when the British empire had begun to fade forever, and the Quebec sovereigntist movement which is still bothering us today had started to put down roots – that Lester Pearson's federal Liberal government finally delivered the present maple leaf flag. Partisans of the old British dominion still raised stiff objections at the time. I vaguely recall that the 1964 flag debate in Ottawa played a sort of noisy counterpoint to my university football band.

There are those who still argue that the maple leaf is not in fact the best symbol of Canada's historic geographic unity and national geographic fact. As best as I can make out, they are probably right. In *The Fur Trade in Canada*, Harold Innis suggests that the birch tree is a more authentic and representative symbol of Canada's national geography than the maple. And the entries for "birch" and "maple" in the much more recent *Canadian Encyclopedia* seem to bear this out.

Canadian soldiers in the First World War, however, had worn

---

*Manitoba and Ontario both retain versions of this old Canadian red ensign as their provincial flags today. And memories of the Union Jack still figure in the provincial flags of British Columbia and Newfoundland.

maple-leaf patches on their shoulders, to distinguish them from other troops of the British empire. In 1921 Canada was "granted" a coat of arms that included maple leaves. The maple leaf figured on the uniforms of Canadian soldiers in the Second World War. For better or worse, it seemed to be the symbol on which the greatest number of federal politicians in the 1960s could agree. Once something of this sort becomes established, I suppose, it's not easy to change.

I've also read somewhere about how, during the flag debate of the 1960s, the president of Ireland told Lester Pearson (who had won the Nobel Prize for Peace in 1957) that a real national flag must have some "blood" on it. Apart from the blood that literally hundreds of thousands of maple-leaf-wearing Canadian soldiers certainly did spill in Europe during the two world wars (and in Korea), nothing of this sort beyond strong language surrounded the proclamation of the new Canadian flag in 1965. But I don't think there are many people in the country today, outside or inside Quebec, who worry a great deal about that.

Canada's "national medicare system"

Flags are, of course, just symbols. There were some more substantial events of the 1960s that marked the fading of the old dominion. They flowed from a quiet recognition that Canada was at last becoming a *real* democracy – which "belonged" to its citizens and, in one way or another, ought to be helping them to live better lives.

To start things off, the pioneering province of Saskatchewan had introduced public hospital insurance in 1945. In the midst of some considerable controversy, it extended the principle to more comprehensive medical insurance in 1962.

In 1957 the federal government at Ottawa established a program to subsidize the costs of provincial hospital insurance schemes. By 1961, all ten Canadian provinces had schemes in place that took advantage of the federal aid. In 1966 the federal government passed legislation that extended its financial support to more comprehensive provincial medical insurance schemes, of the sort established by Saskatchewan in 1962. By 1971 all ten provinces were participating in this program as well.

It seems to me quite absurd to say that the Canadian national medicare system which arose in this way is a key to Canada's present national identity. But for most of us, publicly funded health care probably is one clear advantage of being a citizen of Canada rather than the USA. (And without the historic adventure of the northern North American fur trade, there would be no citizens of Canada to enjoy this advantage today.)

The Canada and Quebec pension plans

In fact, the present national medicare system in Canada is really ten different provincial systems, partly funded by the federal government in Ottawa (and, in the age of balancing the budget and all that, less so lately than used to be the case).

Among other things, this arrangement has allowed the provincial government of Quebec to look after the health care needs of the province's francophone majority in its own language. Another nation-building social program established in the 1960s, however, worked in a different way.

The Canada Pension Plan (CPP) was introduced by the federal government in 1965 (the same year as the new maple leaf flag), and first took effect in 1966. It is an earnings-related public pension scheme that transfers contributions from currently employed workers to retired persons.

I have just been reading up on the tedious bargaining and protracted intergovernmental negotiations of the 1960s that led to the CPP. Without getting into details, the result was a Canada Pension Plan for "Canada outside Quebec," administered by the federal government of Canada, and an identical Quebec Pension Plan (QPP, in English) for residents of that province, administered by the provincial government of Quebec.

In the case of the CPP, contributions from currently employed workers that are not required for current payments to retired persons are invested in provincial government bonds. In the case of the QPP, contributions of this sort are invested in an institution known as the Caisse de dépôt et placement du Québec, which has helped promote the growth of a French-speaking business class in the lower St. Lawrence valley.

This arrangement was negotiated by a Canadian federal Liberal government under Lester Pearson, and a Quebec provincial Liberal government under Jean Lesage. When the broad parameters of the deal were struck in the spring of 1964, Lesage told the Quebec legislature that the one predominantly French-speaking part of Canada had "finally" been "recognized as a province which has a *statut spécial* in Confederation."*

The real truth about Pierre Trudeau

There would be no more deals of this sort after Pierre Trudeau succeeded Lester Pearson as leader of the federal Liberal Party and prime minister of Canada in 1968. In Trudeau's Canada – as in the only slightly earlier Canada of Lester Pearson's immediate predecessor, John Diefenbaker from Prince Albert, Saskatchewan – there would be just one Canadian flag for everyone.

More exactly, Trudeau wanted to make all of the new democracy's vast geographic fact more hospitable to French-speaking Canadians, from coast to coast to coast. If you were going to demand that English-speaking Canada outside Quebec take on this burden, as a matter of justice, you couldn't *also* demand a special status for the province of Quebec itself. That would only perpetrate a new injustice on the rest of the country. (And for a lot of people outside Quebec, it seems to me now, this is exactly what the Meech Lake Accord of 1987 would try to do – with what ought to have been quite predictable results.)

At the same time, even if Trudeau had never come to Ottawa in 1965 and become prime minister in 1968, Canada would likely have experimented with some form of official bilingualism in the 1970s, 1980s, and 1990s. It was Lester Pearson's Liberal government that appointed the Royal Commission on Bilingualism and Biculturalism in 1963. And it was this enterprise that laid

---

*In case anyone is interested, the details of the negotiations and the resulting deal are discussed at length in Richard Simeon, *Federal-Provincial Diplomacy: The Making of Recent Policy in Canada* (Toronto: University of Toronto Press, 1972), Chapter 3.

the formal groundwork for what became Pierre Trudeau's Official Languages Act of 1969.

The so-called "Bye and Bye" commission didn't finally disband until 1971. And I've lately read in the papers that some students of the subject feel the commissioners might have reached out more in the direction of the Canada/Quebec Pension Plan model, if Trudeau hadn't risen to such prominence so quickly. Canada, on this view, would have moved at least closer to language and other policies based on the interests of the *French-speaking majority in Quebec* and the *English-speaking majority in the rest of the country*, rather than the *French-speaking minority in the rest of the country* and the *English-speaking minority in Quebec*.

The implication here is that this could have made everything which followed so much easier. But I'm extremely sceptical myself. I don't think anyone had much of an idea about just where the new aspiring Canadian democratic national state was headed, when it first began to crystallize in the later 1960s.

Trudeau thought he had a clear view of the future, and that was the source of much of his appeal – even in parts of the country where he was not well-liked, personally. All any concerned person in the rest of Canada could hope to understand was that if the new successor to the old dominion were to crash on the rocks, the new Parti Québécois (which René Lévesque had also pulled together by 1968) would be there to pick up the pieces. At least Trudeau seemed to know what he was doing. Say what you like, he *was* a larger-than-life inspiration. And at press conferences, federal-provincial conferences, in the papers, in the streets, on radio and on television, and everywhere else, he could make René Lévesque look small.

Exhibit 16
Population Growth
Canada and Its Provinces and Territories, 1961–1991
(USA Comparison, 1960–1990)

Province/Territory	Population (000s) 1961	1991	Increase (%)
British Columbia	1,629	3,380	107
Alberta	1,332	2,601	95
Ontario	6,236	10,472	68
Quebec	**5,259**	**7,081**	**35**
Newfoundland	458	580	27
Nova Scotia	737	918	25
New Brunswick	598	749	25
Prince Edward Island	105	131	25
Manitoba	922	1,113	21
Saskatchewan	925	1,006	9
Northwest Territories	23	61	165
Yukon Territory	15	29	93
Rest of Canada	**12,979**	**21,039**	**62**
CANADA	18,238	28,120	54
USA	179,323	248,710	39

SOURCES: Statistics Canada, US Bureau of the Census.

Five

JOBS, JOBS, JOBS
(Another interlude)

I'm a Lumberjack and That's Okay

My wife remembers that her grandfather, who had been a classic Canadian prince-of-a-guy lumberjack in his youth, would always say that it was "a great day for Canada" on his birthday. There is something about this habit that strikes me as altogether admirable, and I'd like to work it into my own life. Yet every time my birthday comes around, I seem to forget.

In any case, I do remember talking with my wife's grandfather's eldest son (my father-in-law, as it happens), not too long after Pierre Trudeau's ultimate humiliation of René Lévesque, in the May 1980 Quebec referendum.

Canadian newspapers were full of talk about Trudeau's efforts to "patriate the constitution" from the United Kingdom, in fulfilment of what Trudeau at least regarded as his pledges during the referendum campaign. My father-in-law and I got to talking about all this, over some liquid refreshments out in his backyard, one sunny summer afternoon. And he told me something that I seemed to be hearing again and again, from all sorts of people at the time (and many times since as well).

"It would be nice to have this constitution thing sorted around, I guess," he said. "But our real problem right now is jobs ... the economy and so forth. I can't understand why Trudeau isn't paying a lot more attention to that."

An introduction to the Canadian resource economy

While never a classic Canadian lumberjack himself, my father-in-law did express, I think, a classic Canadian attitude to the never-ending debate on the future of Canada and Quebec (in English and even, to no small extent, in French). And this takes us into another aspect of the fur trade legend that Pierre Trudeau first tried to bring to bear on Canadian public life.

Probably the single most interesting feature of the legend today is how it helps explain the real historical background to the cultural diversity that increasingly marks contemporary Canada.

But the full title of Harold Innis's classic book of 1930 was *The Fur Trade in Canada: An Introduction to Canadian Economic History*. And it was the economic development dimensions of the fur trade in Canada that obsessed the veterans of the First World War and their immediate successors.

In at least one of its economic development dimensions, the fur trade legend is the story of the Canadian resource economy. The fur trade itself does introduce the story in many respects. Yet (in the words of Harold Innis) it was "in the beginning subsidiary to the fishing industry" in "the area tributary to the St. Lawrence River" on the north Atlantic coast. In 1940 Innis published another dense classic on *The Cod Fisheries: The History of an International Economy*.

Fishing remained a key to life on the north Atlantic coast. Meanwhile, from the sixteenth to the early nineteenth centuries, the fur trade carved out the geographic and institutional structure of the Canadian resource economy, from the Atlantic to the Arctic to the Pacific (where another new fishing industry would ultimately succeed the one that was already there).

Then, in the nineteenth and twentieth centuries, the transcontinental system, pioneered by the fur trade, was taken over by lumbering (virtually everywhere but the prairies and the far north), wheat (first in central Canada and then, in its golden age, on the prairies), mining (virtually everywhere again), pulp and paper (allied with lumbering), hydroelectricity (in various places), and oil and natural gas (starting very gently in central Canada and then blossoming boldly in the west and north and even the far east, off the coast of Newfoundland).

A bibliography from the mid-1970s, that Walt once drew to my attention in a used book store, lists more than two dozen minor-classic Canadian books on various branches of this subject. Along with Innis's *Fur Trade* and *Cod Fisheries*, they include Arthur Lower's *The North American Assault on the Canadian Forest* (1938), J.A. Guthrie's *The Newsprint Paper Industry* (1941), Arnold Hoffman's *Free Gold: The Story of Canadian Mining* (1946), Vernon Fowke's *The National Policy and the Wheat Economy* (1957), John H. Dales's *Hydroelectricity and Industrial Development* (1957), and Eric J. Hanson's *Dynamic*

Decade (1958 – an account of "the explosion of the oil and gas industry in Alberta after the Second World War").

The staples thesis and Monty Python

Walt will tell you that at the bottom of the fur trade legend of the Canadian resource economy is the so-called "staples thesis" of Canadian economic development – a subject that used to bore me almost to tears during my own Canadian higher education in the 1960s. I live in a big city, I used to think, and my father works in an office. What does all this have to do with me?

In 1921 more than a third of the Canadian labour force had been directly employed in so-called primary or resource industries (including agriculture). By 1951, this proportion had shrunk to less than 20%. The comparable statistic was less than 6% in the middle of the 1990s.

Lately, one of the local cable channels that my wife and I receive has been rerunning the "Monty Python's Flying Circus" television series from the UK. This was a staple of the English-language Canadian media diet not long after we both graduated from university in the late 1960s. And we still enjoy the "I'm a lumberjack and that's okay" skit – Monty Python's one satirical (and only mildly venomous) bow to the former colonies of the greatest empire since Rome, in northern North America.

The skit could be read, I suppose, as a burlesque of sorts on the 1920s Broadway operetta *Rose Marie*, which celebrated the special atmosphere of the northern North American resource economy in a less-overtly satirical way.

The North West (later Royal Canadian) Mounted Police, who are supposed to have brought order to the northern wilderness as the fur traders gave way to the lumberjacks and miners and wheat farmers and all that, played a role in both cases. But in the Python skit, the rugged Mounties and their lumberjack friends, after a hard day chopping down trees and whatnot, "put on women's clothing and hang around in bars."

In the late 1960s and early 1970s, as best as I can recall, this seemed to sum up my own feelings about the Canadian resource economy almost exactly. And the Python skit can still make me laugh (no doubt because it reminds me of the laughter of my long-lost and much-lamented youth). Yet, partly as a result of having had to earn a living over the past several decades, I now appreciate much more than I used to just how important the resource economy still is in present-day Canada.

Bre-X and the Canadian resource economy today

Though less than 6% of the Canadian labour force is now directly employed in primary industries, there are a lot of other jobs that depend on the resource sector – including many office jobs in various big and smaller cities.

To start with, the northern resource economy has helped make Canada the kind of place that exports a comparatively large share of what it produces. In the mid-1990s, exports accounted for a third or more of the Canadian gross domestic product, compared with around 10% in the United States and Japan, and around one-quarter in the UK, France, Germany, and Italy.* Even now, resource products account for at least a bare majority of all exports in Canada at large, and considerably more than a bare majority outside Ontario and Quebec.

Similarly, a lot of people who work in various communications, financial, service, trade, and transportation industries in Canada today are really just managing the continuing Canadian natural resource base, and living off its export earnings. The Bank of Montreal, which used to call itself "Canada's first bank," was actually founded in the early nineteenth century with profits from the fur trade.

Even at the edge of the twenty-first century, the Toronto, Montreal, Vancouver, and Alberta stock exchanges are still, to no small extent, widely perceived as essentially resource-industry financial markets. And the natural-resource bias of the historic Canadian financial and service sectors is, in a number of respects,

---

*For these statistics and much else in the surrounding pages, I am drawing on a useful article that Ted passed along: P. Cross, F. Roy, C. Bloskie, and D. Pérusse, "Economic Developments in 1995," in Statistics Canada, *Canadian Economic Observer*, April 1996, 3.1– 3.23.

carrying over into the current era of economic globalization.

Many traditional Canadian resource enterprises now have interests and active projects in many different parts of the world, beyond Canada itself. Alas, the collapse of the Bre-X gold bubble in Indonesia, during the early spring of 1997, has all-too-dramatically tarnished this emerging global image of Canada's resource-sector expertise. But there is still much quiet talk about how Canadian financial markets are becoming global centres for the organization and management of the international mining industry. And hopefully, someone or something, in charge somewhere in both the rest of the country and Quebec, is taking some very aggressive steps to ensure that nothing quite like Bre-X ever happens in Canada again.

Exhibit 17
Occupation Structure of the Canadian Labour Force 1921, 1951, 1995

Occupational group	Percentage of labour force in occupational group		
	1921	1951	1995
Primary	36.6	19.8	5.4
Manufacturing	20.8	25.1	15.2
Construction	5.8	6.2	6.0
Transportation	7.8	9.5	7.5
Trade	9.4	10.1	17.1
Services	19.2	28.2	48.8
TOTAL	100.0	100.0	100.0

SOURCE: Statistics Canada.

Exhibit 18
Canadian Exports by Sector
1995

Sector	Exports ($ Millions)	% Value of All Exports
Industrial Goods	47,589.4	19.2
Forestry Products	39,175.4	15.8
Energy Products	22,582.7	9.1
Agricultural and Fishing Products	19,466.6	7.9
RESOURCE SECTORS	**128,814.1**	**52.0**
Automotive Products	61,290.4	24.7
Machinery and Equipment	48,298.8	19.5
Consumer Goods	6,576.1	2.7
Special Transactions	2,728.5	1.1
INDUSTRIAL SECTORS	**118,893.8**	**48.0**
ALL SECTORS	247,703.4	100.0

SOURCE: Statistics Canada.

Exhibit 19
Resource Domination of Export Base
by Province, 1995

Province/Territory	Provincial Resource Exports as a Percentage of All Canadian Resource Exports	Provincial Resource Exports as a Percentage of All Provincial Exports
Newfoundland	1.3	97.5
Saskatchewan	6.6	96.1
New Brunswick	4.0	95.8
Alberta	**19.0**	**92.3**
British Columbia	**18.6**	**89.1**
Prince Edward Island	0.2	75.6
Nova Scotia	1.6	69.0
Manitoba	2.9	67.3
Quebec	**19.3**	**54.9**
Ontario	**26.3**	**27.3**
Territories	0.2	98.0
CANADA	100.0	52.0

SOURCE: Statistics Canada.

15

Canadian Auto Workers, Etc.

On a crisp day last fall, I sat in on an argument between Walt and Ted – at Walt and Madeleine's place, on the Ottawa River. Walt was musing about the great booms of timber that used to float by what is now his front door. Suddenly he said that the Canadian economy had "crucified itself on a cross of natural resources."

Canada was "a mere hewer of wood and drawer of water for more sophisticated economic actors elsewhere – at first in France and Great Britain, and then especially in the USA." And all this probably pointed to one sense in which the legend of the fur trade "had not served Canadians who want jobs all that well."

The strange industrial corollary
of the fur trade in Canada

I could tell from his tone of voice that Walt was only half-serious. But he raised a reaction from Ted (speaking both as a federal civil servant whose job was to be positive about everything, and as someone who had grown up in the Canadian west).

The economic development side of the fur trade legend, Ted argued, wasn't just about the Canadian resource economy. It was also about the creation of Canada's historic geographic unity and "an east-west transcontinental economy," from coast to coast to coast. To help keep this unity alive, after the fur trade had faded, federal government policy in the later nineteenth and earlier twentieth centuries had engineered a strange brand of the industrial revolution in Canada. And some still stranger legacies of this revolution are still more or less thriving today.

Thus, in the middle of the 1990s, the single-largest Canadian commodity export was the "quite unnatural resource of automotive products." Some 48% of all exports came from industrial rather than resource sectors of the aspiring new democracy's "national economy." Industrial sectors accounted for almost 73% of all exports from Ontario, some 45% from Quebec, and close to a third from Manitoba and Nova Scotia.

Ted was starting to enjoy himself. Trade statistics, he went on, didn't lend much support either to a related myth, prominent in some quarters during the debate on Canada-US free trade.

"People like you, Walt," Ted almost shouted, "keep saying that all Americans want from Canada is raw materials. And if this were true, you'd expect to find that the parts of Canada most dependent on resource exports are also the parts of Canada most dependent on export markets in the United States.

"In fact, Ontario and Quebec are the two provinces most dependent on US export markets. And they are also the two provinces where industrial sectors of the economy account for the largest share of exports. The other two big provinces of the confederation, Alberta and British Columbia, are more dependent on resource exports than Ontario and Quebec, and (especially in BC) less dependent on exports to the USA."

The Canadian-American manufacturing syndrome

This last argument brought Walt close to indignation. Nowadays, he pointed out, "the United States buys a lot of Canada's industrial products just because so many of these products are made by Canadian branch plants of US corporations."

The so-called Canadian automobile industry, both Walt and Ted agreed, is probably the most highly developed example of this syndrome. But along with Chrysler Canada, Ford Motor Co. of Canada, and General Motors of Canada, there are also General Electric Canada, Hewlett-Packard (Canada), IBM Canada, ITT Canada, McDonnell Douglas Canada, Rockwell International of Canada, 3M Canada, Westinghouse Canada, and on and on.

The syndrome, Walt continued, is extremely well-known and has almost been studied to death. The early minor classic of the genre, *Canadian-American Industry*, by Herbert Marshall, Frank Southard, Jr., and Kenneth W. Taylor, first appeared in 1936.

It was published as part of a vaguely famous series of books on Canada between the two world wars, funded by the Carnegie Endowment for International Peace in the United States. And the series was effectively presided over by none other than the original Canadian fur-trade guru, Harold Innis.

The best recent study, Walt said, is Glen Williams's some-what confusingly titled, *Not for Export: The International Competitiveness of Canadian Manufacturing*. It first appeared in 1983, with updated and revised editions in 1986 and 1994.

Williams's book explains how the industrial revolution in Canada has leaned on government policies that "transferred northward a share of U.S. production which, although truncated, was roughly proportional to Canada's population." The result has been that at least the industrial part of "the Canadian economy has appeared for some time to be more like a *zone* within the American economy than a distinct national economy." (Or, as Innis himself put it as long ago as 1930, Canada has merely "participated in the industrial growth of the United States" – without ever quite developing an industrial economy of its own.)

The ambiguity of industrial growth in Canada today

Both Walt and Ted also agreed that there have always been some exceptions to the Canadian-American syndrome in Canadian industrial development – home-grown or "indigenous" firms that have done well in both domestic and international markets, inside and outside the USA. And today, some European and Japanese industrial firms locate facilities in Canada, to take advantage of its proximity to the global powerhouse of the American market.

Happily enough, at the edge of the twenty-first century the low value of the Canadian dollar, public health insurance (whose costs must be absorbed by private industry in the US), and Canada-US free trade all help make Canada an attractive enough location for North American manufacturing. Ted noted a recent report that ranked the Toyota plant in Cambridge, Ontario, as the second-most-competitive passenger-car manufacturing facility in the United States and Canada. Four other Canadian facilities also ranked among the twenty most-competitive North American car and truck manufacturing sites, in the same report.

Yet Ted stressed as well that all five of these places were located in Ontario (and even in the greater Toronto region centres of Bramalea, Cambridge, Oakville, and Oshawa). "Whatever else," Ted went on, "it has been a great political and even national weakness of the strange brand of industrial revolution in Canada that the jobs it has provided have been concentrated in Ontario and, to a lesser extent, Quebec."

Walt argued that "this just reflects the historic industrial geography of the adjacent United States." But Ted urged that "even if that's true, it has still tended to limit Canadian enthusiasm for industrial growth, from coast to coast to coast.

"The resource sector in Canada is everywhere, but in many parts of the country, national industrial policy has always just seemed like regional development strategy for Ontario and Quebec." (And this is one reason, Ted went on, "why the Quebec sovereigntist movement has always advocated some form of continuing economic association with the rest of Canada.")

At this point, Walt put an end to the argument with some utterly final thoughts. In Canada, as elsewhere, "the bottom line on traditional industrial growth today is that it just isn't providing many new jobs anywhere, any more." In 1951 some 25% of the Canadian labour force had been employed in manufacturing – up from just over 20% in 1921. But by 1995, the proportion had shrunk to a mere 15%.

Ted had to agree (and so did I). Over the past few decades, Canada has had some success in restructuring its manufacturing sector and making it more efficient. But, as Ted put it, this "just means using more and more sophisticated machinery, to produce more goods more cheaply with fewer workers."

Walt went back to his musings on the great booms of timber that used to float by what is now his front door, on the banks of the Ottawa River, in the exurbs of Canada's national capital region. He still thought "that the old industrial revolution was just a strange and marginal episode in Canadian development." Ted just said: "Well if what you mean is that it's not a place where any sensible person is going to look for 'jobs, jobs, jobs' today, then of course you're right."

Exhibit 20
Exports to the United States by Province, 1994

Province/Territory	Value of Exports to US as Percentage of Value of All Exports
Ontario	**90.6**
Quebec	**81.7**
Alberta	77.2
Nova Scotia	72.0
New Brunswick	71.7
Manitoba	71.5
Prince Edward Island	63.0
British Columbia	**55.9**
Newfoundland	53.4
Saskatchewan	50.7
Territories	6.4
CANADA	**81.1**

SOURCE: Statistics Canada.

Exhibit 21
Exports by Sector
Ontario and British Columbia, 1995

ONTARIO % Value of Exports in Sector		BRITISH COLUMBIA % Value of Exports in Sector	
Automotive Products	44.9	Forestry Products	61.8
Machinery and Equipment	23.7	Industrial Goods	13.6
Consumer Goods	2.9	Energy Products	7.8
Special Transactions	1.2	Agr. and Fishing Products	5.9
INDUSTRIAL	**72.7**	**RESOURCES**	**89.1**
Industrial Goods	17.8	Machinery and Equipment	6.9
Forestry Products	5.5	Automotive Products	1.8
Agr. and Fishing Products	3.4	Consumer Goods	1.5
Energy Products	0.6	Special Transactions	0.7
RESOURCES	**27.3**	**INDUSTRIAL**	**10.9**
ALL EXPORTS	100.0	ALL EXPORTS	100.0

SOURCE: Statistics Canada.

Exhibit 22
Exports by Sector
Quebec and Alberta, 1995

QUEBEC % Value of Exports in Sector		ALBERTA % Value of Exports in Sector	
Industrial Goods	28.6	Energy Products	55.1
Forestry Products	20.7	Industrial Goods	16.3
Agr. and Fishing Products	3.9	Agr. and Fishing Products	13.7
Energy Products	1.7	Forestry Products	7.2
RESOURCES	**54.9**	**RESOURCES**	**92.3**
Machinery and Equipment	28.6	Machinery and Equipment	6.1
Automotive Products	10.2	Special Transactions	0.8
Consumer Goods	5.1	Automotive Products	0.4
Special Transactions	1.2	Consumer Goods	0.4
INDUSTRIAL	**45.1**	**INDUSTRIAL**	**7.7**
ALL EXPORTS	100.0	ALL EXPORTS	100.0

SOURCE: Statistics Canada.

16

The New Economy

Of course, if you really want to worry about "jobs, jobs, jobs" in Canada today, you are also going to have to come to grips with such ponderous new realities as globalization, the information revolution, and the new economy.

As I've noted earlier, just as the age of the canoe and portage once gave way to the age of the railway (which then gave way to the automobile), at the edge of the twenty-first century all the old industrial ages are giving way to a new high-technological era of electronic computers, global telecommunications, and all that.

I read recently (in an item that Ted passed along) how in 1995 – the year of the second sovereignty referendum in Quebec – the three most rapidly growing sectors of the Canadian economy were "electrical and electronic products manufacturing, communications, and business services." The "strength of export demand" for key products in Canada's old-fashioned resource and manufacturing sectors "helped to fuel corporate spending on business services and telecommunications."

The "need for more computer services was the driving force behind the higher demand for business services." And, as all such documents seem to note nowadays, the "increased integration of Canada into the global economy plays a large role in all this."[*]

New high-tech roots in the old economy

It is certainly worth bearing in mind, I think, that recent growth in the Canadian version of the new economy has in fact been fuelled by buoyant exports of more traditional northern North American industrial and resource products.

The Japanese branch plants of Honda Canada Inc., which send automobiles made in Canada to the United States, was the

---

[*]Cross, Roy, Bloskie, and Pérusse, "Economic Developments in 1995," *Canadian Economic Observer*, April 1996, 3.7-3.8.

aspiring new democracy's twelfth-largest exporter in 1995. (The top three, of course, were General Motors of Canada, Chrysler Canada, and Ford Motor Co. of Canada.)

The list of top exporters in 1995 also included such more or less home-grown resource enterprises as Abitibi-Price Inc., Alcan Aluminum Ltd., Avenor Inc., Canadian Pacific Ltd., Domtar Inc., Falconbridge Ltd., Inco Ltd., MacMillan Bloedel Ltd., Noranda Inc., Nova Corp., and even a few government firms like the Canadian Wheat Board and Hydro-Québec.

At the same time, irrepressible optimists will urge that Canada today can lay claims of a sort to at least a few home-grown bright lights in the high-technology new economy as well. And they are, more or less, right. The list here includes Northern Telecom (though everyone always asks, "Is it *really* a Canadian company?"), Bombardier (the star of the new francophone business class in Quebec, mobilized in part by the financial resources of the Quebec Pension Plan), and perhaps such smaller firms as Corel Corp., Mitel Corp., and Newbridge Networks (the facilities for several of which can be viewed on the way to Walt and Madeleines's riverside home, in the Ottawa exurbs).

The underside of the new economy

According to Ted (and I agree), high technology *is* the driving force of the new economy. At the same time, in the middle of the 1990s, about 27% of the employed Canadian labour force was engaged in goods-producing industries (primary or resource production, manufacturing, and construction), and about 73% in service-producing industries (transportation, trade, and a vast assortment of business, community, and other services).

This is quite a dramatic shift from the 1920s, when about 63% of the labour force worked in goods-producing and 37% in service-producing industries. A key feature of the new economy today is that the majority of us now work in one or another form of service industry. And more than a few of the services involved have very little to do with high technology, and a lot to do with intermittent, insecure, and often strangely demanding work in such places as fast-food outlets and telemarketing centres.

A related and much-discussed trend is the decline of long-term employment opportunities or so-called "permanent jobs" in large corporate organizations – in both the private and public sectors of the new economy. As best as I can recall, small business has been touted as the leading creator of new jobs since the later 1970s. Corporate and government downsizing in the somewhat more recent past has also served to swell the ranks of self-employed individuals. In 1995 some 15% of all Canadian workers were self-employed.

Ted says that much of this is just a response to new needs for flexibility and innovation, brought on by the high-technological age of computers, global telecommunications, and all that. I think there is a lot to this point of view. And I think the new economy is bringing some fresh opportunities for leading interesting lives: I have been self-employed myself for close to two decades now, and I like it much better than any other job I've had. But I think that the new economy is also rather clearly creating new challenges for any sane and stable social existence among "family and friends" (which is, at the bottom of everything, it seems to me, what most people mean when they talk so passionately about "jobs, jobs, jobs").

How government ought to work

I've talked with my sister, Veronica, about all of this lately, several times. Something we do seem to agree on is that, over the longer term, governments – and especially national governments – are one of the few forms of present-day human organization that stand any realistic chance of managing the challenges of the new economy effectively, in the interests of the great majority of job-seeking people. (And I think my father-in-law, who wondered why Trudeau didn't pay more attention to jobs and the economy, would probably agree.)

Of course, the immediate impact of such ponderous new realities as globalization and the information revolution has been to present a quite different challenge for the traditional national state. Another new economic trend is the cold passion for balancing the budget, and all that, in the public sector. And, for good enough reasons, this trend has now seized virtually all forms and levels of government in Canada today.

In the Trudeau era, the public sector seemed to be picking up most of the "technological unemployment" that recurrent waves of new economic growth have induced, from the first old industrial revolution in late eighteenth-century Great Britain down to the present. More recently, even Canada has rediscovered the free market and the private sector. The current prevailing wisdom is that so-called direct job creation by governments is not economically creative in the end. And I think there is a lot to be said for this point of view as well.

I also think it's significant, however, that no government in Canada – as in most comparable places elsewhere – has seriously embarked on any wholesale dismantling of the social safety nets that gradually arose after the Great Depression and the Second World War. Ted says that much of the early experience with government activity of this sort has proved in great need of financially responsible restructuring and reform, and I think he's right. But it still seems to me that the direction in which the new economy is heading is ultimately going to require still stronger financially responsible expressions of the underlying principle.

Veronica and I also seem to agree that the challenges of the new economy will ultimately require some much broader re-thinking of how national governments relate to national economies. One of many specific concerns in Canada turns around what presently passes for international trade. Just to dramatize the point, I've heard it said that if the share of all Canadian exports destined for the USA increases over the next thirty years at the same rate that it has increased over the past thirty years, by somewhere around the year 2025 virtually all Canadian exports will be going to the USA.

The present Canadian federal government has made some effort to help diversify Canada's export base in the newly dynamic Asia-Pacific region of the global economy (where British Columbia's resource base, in particular, already has something of a foothold), and in various parts of Latin America. There are, I would certainly agree, reasons to be sceptical about the practical prospects for this kind of national development strategy. Yet I want to end here on the sort of positive note that Veronica's closest friend, Ted, is so keen to encourage. As I've alluded to earlier, it does strike me that the present federal government's trade policy is a small step in the right direction – and, at the very least, much better than doing nothing at all.

Exhibit 23
Top Fifteen Canadian Export Customers, 1995

Country	Exports $ (Millions)	% Value of All Exports
United States	196,160.6	79.2
Japan	11,857.4	4.9
United Kingdom	3,747.8	1.5
China	3,212.2	1.3
Germany	3,150.4	1.3
South Korea	2,695.4	1.1
France	1,887.6	0.8
Belgium	1,823.4	0.7
Italy	1,767.6	0.7
Taiwan	1,683.4	0.6
Netherlands	1,584.0	0.6
Hong Kong	1,377.5	0.6
Brazil	1,265.3	0.5
Australia	1,138.6	0.4
Mexico	1,106.9	0.4
TOP 15	234,458.1	94.7
ALL COUNTRIES	247,703.4	100.0

SOURCE: Statistics Canada.

Six

WHY EVERYONE
HATES ONTARIO
(and the anglophone minority in Quebec)

At the Wedgewood Hotel

I was in Vancouver on business early in June 1990 – not long before the Meech Lake Accord finally collapsed. I'm spiritually attracted to the place. And I often enough think that I'd be happy to take my last breath there, on some rainy autumn afternoon. As someone still from another part of the country, however, I'm also struck by a deep note of irony in the city today.

Vancouver's great charm for me is that it's a familiar and *very* Canadian place (in an English-speaking sense, of course) in a mildly exotic location – still best-captured by the giant and gauntly artistic aboriginal totem poles of Canada's Pacific coast. At the same time, Vancouver seems to me as well a place where the vast fragility of today's aspiring Canadian national democracy, national government, and national economy, all together, lurks somewhat quizzically on almost every city street.

Men in suits talking

On the last day of my June 1990 trip to the city, to take just one of countless examples, I was having a leisurely breakfast in the dining room of the Wedgewood Hotel on Hornby Street, where I had been staying. I was alone at a comfortable table, happily lost in some newspapers. But I found it impossible to ignore an increasingly heated conversation, a few tables away.

Four men in suits were talking. As best as I could figure out, two were from some firm in Toronto and two were from the Vancouver office of the same firm (or perhaps some separate Vancouver firm that regularly did work of some sort for the Toronto firm – or perhaps it was the other way around, and the Toronto office was actually a branch of the Vancouver firm).

In any case, the two men in suits from Vancouver were arguing fiercely with the Toronto pair, about certain aspects of their mutual business. When I left, they were on the verge of physical assault. Back home a few weeks later, when it became clear that the Meech Lake Accord had collapsed, I thought of them again. And it seemed to me that, in some odd way, the demise of Meech Lake had something to do with their argument.

Much more recently, during the 1997 federal election campaign, my thoughts returned to the Wedgewood Hotel. I was watching a television report on the campaign in BC. And it struck me that the real future of the present national economy and national government in Canada has at least as much to do with what happens in Vancouver – and, no doubt, Alberta and so forth – as with what happens in Quebec. (Or, another aggravating aspect of our current Canadian confusion is that, as is often-enough said, there is no such thing as a homogeneous English Canada, that might serve as some coherent partner for an at least much more homogeneous French Quebec.)

Regional alienation

Everyone who pays a lot of attention to Canadian public life today has some sense of what this issue is all about. As Ted says, "It touches several different emotional hot buttons." Some think the emotional reaction tends to be much greater than the facts of the case warrant. But that, in itself, is a kind of emotional reaction to the facts of the case.

The most common label for what's involved is western alienation. And the issue is so often cast in these terms because the four provinces of western Canada together – with some special emphasis on the two most-populous and rapidly growing far western provinces of Alberta and BC – are now an increasingly influential home to more than 8.5 million people (or just under 30% of the total Canadian population).

Western Canadians, however, are just the most politically potent exponents of grievances that have echoes almost everywhere in Canada, outside a vague chunk of geography glibly characterized as "the Toronto–Ottawa–Montreal triangle." There is a parallel form of regional alienation in the four provinces of Atlantic Canada. But in the mid-1990s, there were also less than 2.5 million Atlantic Canadians, and the region's *relative share* of the total Canadian population has been declining virtually since the start of the 1867 confederation. This is not to say that

Atlantic Canada's *absolute population* has not been growing. The place was home to only 1.9 million people in 1961. Yet for generations now, Atlantic Canada has been growing much more slowly than western Canada, and its voice of regional alienation is inevitably not so demanding and strong.*

There is a still weaker variation on the theme among the less than 100,000 people in Canada's present two northern territories – almost half of whom are of aboriginal descent. As Walt points out, if you really want to get complicated, there is also some degree of northern alienation in virtually every geographically large Canadian province (which is to say, "Newfoundland and Labrador," Quebec, Ontario, and all of western Canada).

Walt's background on the Laurentian thesis

Of course, every country in the world of any geographic size is subject to some form of regional tension and even political conflict. But Ted says that Canada's particular case of regional neurosis has at least two distinguishing features.

One is the vast number of complicated ways in which the French-speaking majority in Quebec has influenced the wider growth of Canadian federalism outside Quebec, ever since the confederation of 1867 or even before. The other is a controversial history of a particular kind of national economic development. According to Walt, this history has been debated among the English-speaking Canadian historians of the past half-century or so via a somewhat exotic concept known as the Laurentian thesis.

Walt is a critic of the thesis. But he notes that it's famous enough to rate an entry in *The Canadian Encyclopedia* which the Edmonton publisher Mel Hurtig brought out in the 1980s. And here the leading exponent is identified as the University of Toronto historian Donald Creighton, who is said to have drawn on "the staple theory" of Canadian development "advanced by H.A. Innis, particularly in *The Fur Trade in Canada*."

---

*My wife would also rudely point out that "the Atlantic provinces have been bought off by equalization payments." At her urging, I will deal with this particular subject in more detail shortly.

Walt says that what Donald Creighton actually did with Innis's crystallizing work on the Canadian fur trade legend was similar to what Marshall McLuhan did with Innis's later work on empire and communications in world history. Creighton took a few elements in a complex historical pattern and over-simplified them, arriving at a rather artificial message that virtually contradicts what really lies at the bottom of Innis's own highly subtle and open-ended thoughts on the Canadian past.

Alas, not long after Creighton's first book, *The Commercial Empire of the St. Lawrence*, appeared in 1937, Innis became obsessed by the much vaster problems of communications in world history, and then died prematurely from prostate cancer in 1952. Creighton, who lived on until 1979, published a short biographical sketch of Innis in 1957. And this is still the only study of its sort available today (though Walt tells me that someone is currently working on a more suitable replacement).

The upshot of all this is that the real legend of the fur trade has often been confused with and even mistakenly discredited by the Laurentian thesis. Yet according to Walt (who actually does talk this way from time to time), "What the University of British Columbia geographer Cole Harris does, in the 1987 first volume of the *Historical Atlas of Canada*, is much closer to the real meaning of the fur trade legacy for the twenty-first century than anything in the work of Donald Creighton and his disciples."

A quick and dirty sketch

If you keep this sort of qualification in mind, Walt says that the entry in *The Canadian Encyclopedia* – written by A. Brian McKillop, from Carleton University in Ottawa – does serve to clarify just what the Laurentian thesis itself is all about.

To start with, "Creighton argued that Canadian economic and national development derived fundamentally from the gradual exploitation of key staples products ... by colonial merchants in the major metropolitan centres of the St. Lawrence River system" (i.e., Montreal and then later, Toronto).

The major markets for the staples (or natural resource) products were in Europe. In searching out ever-new supplies of these products, the merchants of Montreal ultimately pieced together Canada's present-day national geography – arranging and equipping increasingly more elaborate journeys by canoe and portage along the east-west interior waterways, that stretched from coast to coast to coast.

Thus the system created by the St. Lawrence merchants "provided the basis by which both a transatlantic and a transcontinental market economy could be organized." And in "stressing the connection with the metropolitan capitals of Europe Creighton undermined the continentalism implicit in American historian Frederick Jackson Turner's frontier thesis."

As in the real legend, the spread of the fur trade, under the ultimate guidance of the Montreal-based North West Company, pioneered the Canadian empire of the St. Lawrence. Then, the Montreal-headquartered Canadian Pacific Railway, completed in 1885, "marked an extension of the potential for national development inherent in the St. Lawrence system," and adapted the empire to the new industrial age of steam (and the new resource economies of lumbering, wheat, mining, and so forth).

Finally, by the early twentieth century the merchants of Toronto, at the western end of the St. Lawrence system, had become, as it were, co-conspirators of the merchants of Montreal. And, to bring the story down to at least something quite close to the present, at some point after the Second World War the commercial leadership of the Laurentian empire passed from Montreal to Toronto. Meanwhile, the federal capital in Ottawa remains, above all else, a place where conflicts between the rival central Canadian metropolitan centres are ultimately resolved. And in the very end, regional alienation is just a deep sense of not being at the centre of what counts in Canada, somehow felt by virtually everyone who lives outside the two central and most-populous provinces of Ontario and Quebec. (Or more exactly, perhaps, outside the Toronto–Ottawa–Montreal triangle: And, well, all this is almost certainly something of an exaggeration, but you probably know what I mean.)

Exhibit 24
Ten Largest Canadian Metropolitan Centres, 1921

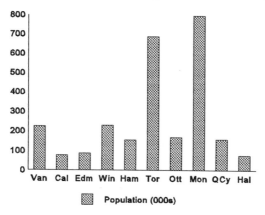

SOURCE: Statistics Canada.

Exhibit 25
Ten Canadian Metropolitan Centres, 1991

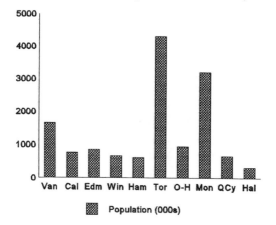

SOURCE: Statistics Canada.

119

18

Autopsy on the Laurentian Thesis

According to many who think about such things today, Walt says, the current bottom line on the Laurentian thesis is that, apart from anything else, the thesis itself is now obsolete.

In theory, this could mean that the various brands of Canadian regional alienation which have arisen in reaction to the thesis (or to what it claims to describe) are obsolete as well. But Ted says that, whatever may or may not be true about the Laurentian thesis itself, the obsolescence of regional alienation in Canada is at best only half-true and at worst not true at all. In some ways regional alienation is now worse than it has ever been before.

The free trade argument about obsolescence

As both Walt and Ted agree, the current argument about the *recent* obsolescence of the Laurentian thesis owes almost everything to the apparent fate of the great international debate of the 1980s and 1990s on free trade – and its various more particular permutations in Canada (or Canada and Quebec, or even Canada, Mexico, and the United States).

On this view, the Canada-US FTA of the late 1980s, NAFTA, the negotiations under the General Agreement on Tariffs and Trade that led to the establishment of the World Trade Organization (WTO) in 1995, and, more recently still, the prospective Multilateral Agreement on Investment (MAI), among the globe's most developed industrial economies, have all effectively outlawed certain kinds of protectionist government trade policies. And it is exactly these kinds of now-outlawed policies which have created and sustained the pattern of Canadian economic growth that the Laurentian thesis describes.

In the more ancient Canadian past (Walt says) this points to the essentially anti-free-trade mercantilist designs of the earliest French and British empires. In more recent Canadian history, it takes us back to the so-called National Policy of tariff protection and transcontinental railway building that John A. Macdonald's founding Canadian federal government put in place – and to certain related, somewhat later Imperial Preference arrangements within the British empire. (And, by the way, one of the particular strange creations of this stream in national policy has been the Canadian-American industrial manufacturing sector, concentrated in Quebec and, especially, in Ontario.)

For better or worse, all the new international trade agreements of the late twentieth century envision a world economy in which national governments forego policies of this sort, in the interests of the greater dynamism that one kind of economic theory attributes to free or at least freer trade.

Another argument: Harold Innis on the change from British to American imperialism in Canada

Ted's view of all this is that there are more than a few reasons to wonder about the long-term stability of the new international trading regimes of the late twentieth century. Yet for the moment, "and perhaps forever, this may not have a lot to do with Canada." To both Walt and Ted, recent Canadian economic development does seem to have been proceeding in such a way as to confirm the argument that the Laurentian thesis *is* obsolete. And this can be read as implying that, in some parts of the world, the new international trading regimes are having their intended effects.

According to Walt, however, the still deeper truth is that economic development in Canada had begun to move in its present directions long before the free trade debates of the 1980s. "If the Laurentian theorists had paid more attention to Harold Innis's evolving views on *current* Canadian growth, in the 1920s, 1930s, and 1940s, they might have grasped more clearly what he was actually saying in *The Fur Trade in Canada*. And then they would have understood that the Laurentian thesis was obsolete almost as soon as it was invented, between the two world wars."

As long ago as the early summer of 1938, Innis was telling an academic conference at the University of Maine about how "Canada is facing to an increasing extent the effects of contrast between two systems." An "old system linked her to Europe by a geographic background dominated by the St. Lawrence." A "new system links Canada to the United States and is evident in the increasing importance of exports from Canada to the United States, such as pulp and minerals, and in the rapid spread of inventions from the United States to Canada ... The radio crosses boundaries which stopped the press."

The old system had everything to do with a Canada that still saw itself as a part of the global trading bloc of the British Empire and Commonwealth. But with the new system in mind, Innis tried to tell his audience in Maine about the parallel emergence of "an American empire without the desire to assume responsibilities that go with imperialism." A decade later, in 1948, he was more boldly telling another academic audience at the University of Nottingham, in the United Kingdom, about the "change from British imperialism to American imperialism" in Canada – which "has been accompanied by friction and a vast realignment of the Canadian system."

Walt's judgement on the thesis itself

According to Walt, Harold Innis parted company with the likes of Donald Creighton as well, in his much sharper appreciation of how the Canadian Laurentian empire of the late nineteenth and early twentieth centuries was only one transient figure on a much broader canvass of northern North American development. Deep in the more ancient Canadian past, the rivalry between English traders on Hudson's Bay and French traders in the St. Lawrence valley had foreshadowed the limits of Laurentian domination over the national geography created by the northern fur trade.

As Innis would also explain in the late 1940s, very early on in the history of the 1867 confederation, the rising United States of America began to have "an increasing influence" on the "east-west system" that had earlier linked Canada "to Great Britain and Europe." From the start, in "the East, Nova Scotia had regarded Confederation as a device for opening American markets, whereas the St. Lawrence region thought of it as a basis of protection against American goods." Then on the eve of the First World War, the completion of "the Panama Canal, through the energetic efforts of Theodore Roosevelt," was "followed by the development of Vancouver as a port competitive with Montreal and by a weakening of the importance of the St. Lawrence."

When the Panama Canal opened for business in the summer of 1914, Innis went on to explain, "Alberta, with its vast potential resources" was just beginning its career as a Canadian province. (Innis himself worked briefly as a rural schoolteacher in northern Alberta.) A generation later, the stupendous, never-ending rock of the Canadian Shield back east, "which has been a handicap to a system built up in relation to Europe, has become a great advantage as a centre for the development of hydro-electric power and for the growth of a pulp and paper and of a mineral industry in relation to the United States."

The bottom line to all this, Walt says, is the dynamism in the most westerly parts of western Canada today. If Canada were in fact *just* a place organized around the particular interests of Ontario and Quebec – as a kind of turned-inside-out version of the Laurentian thesis would imply – how did Alberta and British Columbia ultimately emerge as the country's most dynamic and rapidly growing provinces after the Second World War?

And of course there is another obvious fly in the ointment, Walt points out, "from the standpoint of Madeleine's French-Canadian grandmother." Insofar as some form of central Canadian national conspiracy really has been *one* element in Canada's past, Quebec francophones have never felt that *they* were among its beneficiaries. Since the time of la conquête, the merchants of the old Canadian economic capital in Montreal were overwhelmingly English-speaking. And in this sense, there has been a culturally and linguistically charged version of regional alienation, even in the central Canadian province of Quebec.

From this angle, the beneficiaries of the Laurentian design for Canada reduce to the anglophone minority in Quebec (heavily concentrated around Montreal) and Canada's most-populous province of Ontario. And in the 1930s, Harold Innis, who grew up on a family farm in southwestern Ontario and then spent most of his adult life in Toronto, wrote a short "introduction to an introduction to the economic history of Ontario," which ended on a rather critical note of this sort. "The elasticity of the economy of Ontario," Innis argued, "has been obtained in part through inelastic developments which bear with undue weight on less favoured areas of the Dominion. The strength of Ontario may emphasize the weakness of the federation. An empire has its obligations as well as its opportunities."

Canada as a coalition of regional economies today

Walt says that there is still something to all this, even with the new international trade agreements of the late twentieth century. Broadly speaking, Alberta and BC have been growing more rapidly than Ontario for more than a generation now. But Alberta's most recent population growth, in the first half of the 1990s, has slowed down somewhat, while Ontario has continued to put weight on its status as Canada's most-populous province. Ontario still has the single-largest chunk of even the Canadian resource economy. And, thanks in no small part to the strange industrial corollary of the fur trade in Canada, it still has a considerably more diversified economic base than any other part of the country (with the partial exception of parts of Quebec).*

Dependence on resource exports creates an array of classic problems for any regional economy. And both Walt and Ted agree that, since the middle of the nineteenth century, Canada has in some degree evolved so as to let Ontario get out from under at least the worst of these problems, to a much greater extent than any other Canadian province (again, with the partial exception of Quebec). In this sense, regional alienation isn't just a feeling of not being part of what really counts in central Canada: it's also an intellectual conviction that one's regional interests are not being properly served by the complex processes through which national policy decisions are made.

Ted points out as well that in some ways this phenomenon is now worse than it has ever been before, *because of* "the vast

---

*Again, here you can point most obviously to what remains of the Montreal-centred anglophone minority in Quebec today. At the same time, the rise of a new Quebec francophone business class, on the back of the quiet revolution, has also given some French-speaking Quebecers a new degree of complicity in what may or may not remain of the central Canadian conspiracy.

realignment of the Canadian system" that Harold Innis was already drawing attention to in the late 1940s. And Walt agrees that, if you carefully scrutinize what Innis had to say about the fate of the economic development side of the Canadian fur trade legend in the 1930s and 1940s, what you start to see is a rough sketch of Canada's evolution into a kind of coalition of regional economies. The coalition is still tied together by the historic geographic logic of Canada's founding fur trade era, but it is increasingly divorced from the more particular economic logic of the "old system" which "linked her to Europe by a geographic background dominated by the St. Lawrence."

It was also this vastly realigning new Canada, Walt and Ted both agree as well, that was finally compelled by circumstances to start setting aside the old British dominion after the Second World War, and at last confront the challenges of creating its own new national democracy, head on. It was this new Canada that allowed French-speaking Quebec to reinvent itself in the quiet revolution – and facilitated a movement for a still more sovereign Quebec in the regional politics of the lower St. Lawrence valley. And it was equally this new Canada that finally embraced its own new maple leaf flag, in February 1965.

In this same setting, Ted says, "The crucial problem for national economic policy in Canada today is not really that the new international trade agreements of the late twentieth century have made any such policy virtually illegal. As the Harold Innis who spent the last decade of his life obsessed by the problems of empire and communications in world history would appreciate, Canada's accession to the new trade agreements is just a way of at last trying to fit its own new vastly realigned national system into a vastly realigning international economy."

As Ted sees it (and Walt says that he "would at least like to agree"), the crucial problem is that the evolution of our thinking about national economic policy has just not kept pace with the evolution of Canada's real national economy – which *is* increasingly a coalition of regional economies, more and more and more divorced from the linkages of the old St. Lawrence system. "We are still waiting," Ted says, "for some accompanying vast realignment here."

Exhibit 26
The Change from British Imperialism to American Imperialism

*A Century of Canadian Exports
to the United Kingdom and the United States*

Year	% Value of Exports to United Kingdom	% Value of Exports to United States
1896	57.2	34.4
1916	60.9	27.1
1926	38.5	36.4
1937	38.4	41.0
1946	25.8	40.1
1952	17.3	53.6
1961	15.8	54.0
1974	6.0	65.9
1985	2.0	78.5
1995	1.5	79.2

SOURCES: F.R. Scott, *Canada Today* (1938); *Canada Year Book* (various years); Statistics Canada.

19

Section 36(2) and All That

The last time I was in Ottawa, Veronica told me that Walt's only lukewarm assent to Ted's views on current Canadian national economic policy flows from the special linkages between social and economic policy in Canada today.

Put another way, Walt argues that for some people the truth about the vastly realigned Canadian economic system is that "national policy in this setting is essentially social policy." There is no longer any point to national economic policy in John A. Macdonald's old sense. Or, in Canada today national economic policy *is* just national social policy, and cannot be anything else.

Regional development in Trudeau's new constitution

Ted says that he does agree with Walt to some extent here, at least in the sense that this is how some people do seem to see things in Canada today. And, Ted claims, a case in point is section 36(2) of Pierre Trudeau's new Constitution Act, 1982:

> Parliament and the government of Canada are committed to the principle of making equalization payments to ensure that provincial governments have sufficient revenues to provide reasonably comparable levels of public services at reasonably comparable levels of taxation.

Walt also goes on to argue that this constitutionally mandated requirement for "equalization payments" in Canada (arguably a somewhat strange thing to find in a national constitution in the first place) has arisen in response to criticisms that have a lot to do with the Laurentian thesis. On this view, the federal commitment to ensure reasonably comparable levels of provincial government services is intended to compensate for the injustices otherwise perpetrated on the rest of the country by the Toronto–Ottawa–Montreal triangle. And, as Walt puts it, "Among many official supporters of what Harold Innis called Canadian institutions today, this commitment ranks right up with the national medicare system, as a defining feature of the present Canadian national identity."

One member of the federal parliament, Walt has told Veronica, recently declared that the "equalization program marks our compassion as a nation," symbolizes the very "essence of Canada," and explains "why this country remains united." Another federal MP added that "the equalization program as we know it embodies some of the great ideals and the great values of Canadians," which "all of us cherish ... under our democracy."*

Here again, however, both Walt and Ted more or less agree on at least a few particular problems with the principle of federal government equalization payments to what Ted calls "needy provincial governments." (As it happens, Veronica seems to disagree with both of them. But because she is my sister, I suppose, I almost always pay less attention to her than I do to Walt and Ted – though I also sometimes wonder about this: perhaps my view of Veronica is wrong.)

The conspiracy theory of equalization payments

Walt and Ted say that there are some indirect senses in which the principle of equalization payments probably does embody a noble ideal. Yet viewing it as the "very essence" of Canada, as Walt puts it, "is at best a small-minded approach to defining the great values of our democracy, from coast to coast to coast."

For individual citizens, this conception of the country denigrates the proposition that *Canada's vast geography now belongs to you* (and that *you* can use this geography to fulfil your own dreams). It implies instead that, at the bottom of everything, the Canadian national state is just a regional conspiracy which has the good manners to pay-off its victims.

As Ted explains, "The national commitment in this sense

---

*Walt notes that the individuals involved were George Proud (Hillsborough, on Prince Edward Island) and John Harvard (Winnipeg St. James), as cited in the Queen's University economist Dan Usher's *The Uneasy Case for Equalization Payments* (Vancouver: The Fraser Institute, 1995), 2.

merely means that if you happen to reside in a region which is exploited by the conspiracy, then the federal government will reasonably compensate your provincial government, so that your provincial government can provide you with services reasonably comparable to the services you would get if you resided in the heartland of the conspiracy."

This, no doubt, does embody a certain notion of fairness. Yet, as Ted also likes to explain, "when elevated to the status of 'why this country remains united,' it is not the mark of a national community that intends to do anything of much consequence or imagination with its vast geography." (And Walt's corollary here is that it's "not the mark of a national community that intends to do anything of much consequence at all.")

Who gives and who gets equalization payments, as a test of the Laurentian thesis

Veronica says that Walt and Ted have got things all wrong. Federal-provincial "equalization," in her view, is not supposed to be a guilt payment for any kind of regional alienation, or anything like that. It just reflects a fundamental commitment to some rough and partial degree of equality, in distributing the advantages and benefits of Canadian national life.

Ted says that this may be the ultimate moral argument for equalization, but the politics are different. And he points to an argument of Walt's, that relates back to the Laurentian thesis.

Of course, Walt explains, section 36(2) of the Constitution Act, 1982 did not initiate the practice of equalization payments. In some vague respects, the practice dates back to the earliest days of the 1867 confederation, when Nova Scotia threatened to repeal its accession to the new Dominion of Canada, and then settled for a so-called "better terms" increase in federal subsidies.

The modern Canadian equalization system, however – via a complex mathematical formula that takes an entire page of paper to describe – is a more explicit creation of the period since the Second World War, when the old dominion was giving way to the new national state. And it is rooted philosophically in a view of Canada that has a lot to do with the Laurentian thesis.

Yet, if the Laurentian thesis were even an essentially correct account of the mainstream in Canadian economic development, Walt argues, then one would expect the modern equalization system to transfer federal tax dollars from Ontario and Quebec to the eight provinces of Atlantic and western Canada.

In fact, what the equalization system of the late twentieth-century aspiring Canadian democracy actually does is transfer federal tax dollars *from* Ontario, British Columbia, and Alberta *to* all four provinces of Atlantic Canada, two provinces in western Canada, and the province of Quebec.

Why *should* BC and Alberta pay?

According to Ted, the plot just twists and thickens from this point on. Equalization payments work out the way they do because – again, contrary to what one might deduce from a simple-minded reading of the Laurentian thesis – the most prosperous provinces spawned by the vastly realigned Canadian system of the late twentieth century are not the old St. Lawrence provinces of Quebec and Ontario, but the central and far-western provinces of Ontario, Alberta, and British Columbia.

At the same time, there are still key differences between Ontario on the one hand, and BC and Alberta on the other. Ontario has a more diversified economic base, and depends much more on manufacturing. BC and Alberta have much more resource-dependent economies, in a traditional Canadian sense.

Thus, even if you set the Laurentian thesis aside, Ted claims, you can still argue that Ontario's present economic diversification remains a legacy of certain central Canadian imperialist policies put in place by earlier federal governments. As Harold Innis also noted in his critical mid-1930s essay on Ontario economic history, "An empire has its obligations as well as its opportunities." And this is the kind of political argument that Ontario finally acknowledged when it accepted the principle of federal-provincial equalization, after the Second World War.

Certainly in their own estimation, on the other hand, BC and Alberta have never been the beneficiaries of any national economic policy tilted especially in their direction. They have never been at the centre of any kind of Canadian national empire, organized around their particular interests. Their prosperity has simply flowed from their unusually fortunate natural-resource endowments (as is also true enough, Ted argues, of one but *not* another side of Ontario). So what is the political argument that convinces Alberta and BC to transfer its tax dollars to all four provinces of Atlantic Canada, two provinces in western Canada, and the province of Quebec? Ted's view is that, in the very end, there just isn't any convincing argument of this sort at all.

Exhibit 27
Net Gain or Loss from Equalization Payments, 1994

Province	Net Gain or Loss ($ per person)
Newfoundland	1,385.90
Prince Edward Island	1,089.35
New Brunswick	964.19
Nova Scotia	709.65
Manitoba	551.89
Saskatchewan	309.39
Quebec	280.03
British Columbia	**-280.61**
Alberta	**-287.47**
Ontario	**-317.55**

SOURCE: Usher, *Uneasy Case for Equalization Payments* (1995), 23.

Exhibit 28
Net Gain or Loss from All Federal Transfers, 1994

Province	Net Gain or Loss ($ per person)
Newfoundland	1,823.92
Prince Edward Island	1,515.70
New Brunswick	1,355.72
Nova Scotia	910.32
Manitoba	849.23
Saskatchewan	738.25
Quebec	187.88
Alberta	**-9.64**
British Columbia	**-422.20**
Ontario	**-532.31**

SOURCE: Usher, *Uneasy Case for Equalization Payments* **(1995), 23.**

Seven

THE DEATH OF
THE NATIONAL BUSINESS
CLASS
(and why it may not be such a bad thing)

20

The Museum on Rue Saint-Jacques

One of several new directions that Canada today needs to discover, Ted says, is a national economic policy that does give BC and Alberta some self-interested motivation to play the roles they already play in the federal-provincial equalization system – and in Canadian national social policy at large.*

And here Ted argues as well that, in the long run, there can be no safe and secure Canadian national social policy without some form of supporting national economic policy.

Walt's at least tentative view on this branch of the subject is that Ted has "an interesting intellectual argument. But it ignores what really happens in history." Ultimately, Walt says, "A workable national economic policy can only be developed by (or in conjunction with) a national business class."

The great problem of this sort in Canada today – and this is also, according to Walt, what many people *really* mean when they talk about the obsolescence of the Laurentian thesis – is that the "national" business class the country used to have is now, for all practical purposes, dead, or at best, on its very last legs. Given the nature of the vastly realigned new Canadian economic system, no new national business class is likely to arise to replace the old one. And that is why Canada no longer has, or can have, *any* national economic policy of real consequence.

A summer night in downtown Montreal

When I first heard Walt's argument here, not too long ago now, I was reminded of a trip to Montreal that my wife and I and our three sons took, during the summer after the October 1995 sovereignty referendum. We've been on several Montreal excursions over the past few decades, but this time the memory

---

*Especially in related transfers of federal funds to provincial governments for health care and social welfare programs.

of the October referendum gave the experience a fresh edge.

One evening, about halfway through the trip, we'd been out for dinner in the old city. I felt a sudden urge to explore what is now officially known as Rue Saint-Jacques – the former St. James Street: headquarters of the once imperious anglophone merchants, in the now long-vanished era when Montreal was the undisputed economic capital of Canada.

We made our way at a leisurely pace from Place Jacques-Cartier, west to the haunting towers of the landmark Notre Dame Catholic church (or Basilique Notre-Dame, as today's official *Guide Touristique* has it).* The church, which dates from the late 1820s, looks out onto Place d'Armes, bounded on the south by Rue Notre-Dame, and on the north by Rue Saint-Jacques. In the same vicinity, on the north side of Rue Saint-Jacques, are the offices of the *Montreal Gazette*, which has been English-speaking Montreal's leading newspaper for longer than anyone alive today can remember.

Just west of Place d'Armes, and also on the north side of Rue Saint-Jacques, is the old head office of the Bank of Montreal, constructed in 1847 on what, the *Guide Touristique* explains, was "longtemps appelé le «Wall Street» du Canada." Somewhat further west, on the south side of the street, is the old head office of the Royal Bank of Canada, constructed in 1928 and "au moment de sa construction, l'immeuble le plus élevé de l'Empire britannique" (though this was a distinction soon expropriated, others would stress, by the old head office of the Canadian Bank of Commerce on King Street in Toronto).

Rue Saint-Jacques was almost silent on the night we explored its street-lit shadows. Many of the buildings today are in various tell-tale states of transition and decline. In between the old Royal Bank and Bank of Montreal head offices is a renovated structure that tries to bridge the gap between the past and the future, known as the Centre de commerce mondial de Montréal. But the act is not quite convincing. Rue Saint-Jacques in the very late twentieth century has the atmosphere of a museum. Whatever it

---

*Named after a more famous church in Europe, of course, as are so many landmarks in Canada and so many other parts of the new world.

may have been, it is hardly the "Wall Street of Canada" now.

On the south side of the street, west of Place d'Armes, I noticed a tweedy-looking bar, with a quaint sign hanging perpendicular to the front door. One side read Tavern Saint-Jacques, the other, St. James Tavern (or something like that). It was still early in the evening, but the place was closed up as tight as a drum. It seemed to me the last true survivor of the old St. James Street. I imagined (with what degree of accuracy I have absolutely no idea) that old men with British imperial moustaches met there for lunch, and lamented the pace of change.

The new francophone business class in Quebec

Some of course say it is the Quebec sovereigntist movement that has killed the dynamism of the old economic capital of Canada in Montreal. In such places as Toronto and Calgary today, you can find old anglophone Montrealers who will gladly offer various forms of corroboration for stories of this sort.

According to both Ted and Walt, it is more apt to say that Quebec's 1960s quiet revolution worked hard to promote the growth of a new francophone regional business class. Its destiny has been to challenge the old anglophone commercial ascendancy among the province's French-speaking majority, bequeathed by la conquête. And the success of firms like Bombardier testifies that these efforts have not been altogether in vain. The old economic capital of Canada has given way to a more authentically bilingual and bicultural regional metropolis, somewhat hesitantly celebrated in such English-language Canadian books of the 1980s as *Quebec Inc.* and *Montréal:The New Cité.*

It is true enough that certain vestiges of Montreal's historic role in Canada at large still survive. Ted notes that Canada-wide trucking statistics provide a rough handle on what's been happening lately to the old Canadian east-west economic system, which the merchants of Montreal did so much to pioneer. The official Statistics Canada publication on Canada-wide trucking movements in 1993 reports that Quebec still has the "lowest proportion" of so-called "intra-regional tonnage recorded in the country." More domestic truck movements originating in Quebec, that is to say, wind up in other parts of the country than in any of Atlantic Canada, western Canada, or even Ontario.*

Both Ted and Walt also agree, however, that such statistical vestiges of old imperial grandeur are nothing like the empire itself, when its grandeur still prevailed. The vestiges do help explain why, right from the start of René Lévesque's Parti Québécois, even the Quebec sovereigntist movement has expressed interest in some continuing association with the rest of Canada or the "Canadian economic space." Yet the new bilingual regional business elite in Montreal cannot hope to *rule* over any Canada-wide empire ever again. And this helps account for the still troublesome problems of economic adjustment that are so impossible not to notice, even when you just visit the city today.

Toronto's ambiguous takeover of the Laurentian empire

Another way of looking at what has happened to Montreal, of course, is just to say that the central-western metropolis of Toronto took over the leadership of the Canadian national empire of the St. Lawrence, quite a long time ago.

Walt once showed me some papers from the 1942 annual meeting of the Canadian Historical Association, held during the 300th anniversary of the founding of Montreal. I was struck by some comments in rudimentary French from Harold Innis's friend, Arthur Lower: "En Canada il est certain que Montréal a été notre centre métropole pendant toute notre histoire, dominant le Canada jusqu'au Pacifique. Mais, aujourd'hui il y a des influences qui disputent avec Montréal sa place."

One of these influences, according to Walt, was the amalgamation of the old Standard Mining Exchange and the old Toronto Stock Exchange, to form the modern Toronto Stock Exchange, in the middle of the 1930s. A half-century later, in the 1980s, no less an authority than the president of France would note on a Canadian visit that Toronto (not Montreal) was the "financial

---

*See: Statistics Canada, *Trucking in Canada 1993* (Ottawa: Minister of Industry, December 1995), 46; and Exhibit 29 at the end of this section.

capital of Canada." As I think I may have already alluded to, Toronto had surpassed Montreal as Canada's most-populous metropolitan region by the middle of the 1970s. And while, as recently as 1993, comparatively speaking, somewhat fewer domestic truck movements originating in Ontario were still winding up in other parts of the country than in Quebec, trucking in Ontario remains considerably more dependent on the Canadian national market than in either of Atlantic or western Canada.

At the same time, one great irony of Toronto's modern conquest of Montreal's old central metropolitan status in the Canadian national economy, after the Second World War, is that by the time it had been properly consolidated, the east-west Canadian national economy itself ("linked ... to Europe by a geographic background dominated by the St. Lawrence") had begun to disappear. Walt says, as well, that the deepest truth here is even more subtle, ironic, and cunningly twisted again.

Montreal had been a colonial outpost of the old British global financial centre in London, England. Though Toronto was a decidedly *"British* American" place in the earlier twentieth century, it was also an outpost of the new American global financial centre in New York City. And the rise of Toronto in the second half of the twentieth century was itself part of the "vast realignment of the Canadian system" that Harold Innis wrote about in the late 1940s (brought on by the "change from British imperialism to American imperialism").

In the end, Toronto never exactly *took over* Montreal's historic role in the Canadian economy. Its ultimate triumph just set the stage for the death of the Canadian "national" business class that Montreal had pioneered.

Exhibit 29
Canadian For-hire Trucking in Canada Percentage of Revenues from Province or Region Generated in Canada Outside That Province or Region, 1993

Province/Region of Origin	% Revenues Generated in Canada Outside Province/Region
Newfoundland	38
Prince Edward Island	100
Nova Scotia	55
New Brunswick	55
ATLANTIC REGION	26
QUEBEC	49
ONTARIO	46
Manitoba	72
Saskatchewan	55
Alberta	50
PRAIRIE REGION	37
BRITISH COLUMBIA	38

SOURCE: Statistics Canada.

Exhibit 30
Metropolitan Rivalry in Central Canada
Population Growth, 1901–1991

Year	Population (000s)		Toronto/
	Montreal	Toronto	Montreal
1901	415	303	.73
1911	**616**	**478**	**.70**
1921	796	686	.86
1931	**1,086**	**901**	**.83**
1941	1,216	1,002	.82
1951	**1,539**	**1,264**	**.82**
1961	2,216	1,919	.87
1971	**2,743**	**2,628**	**.96**
1981	2,828	2,999	1.06
1991	**3,213**	**4,036**	**1.26**

SOURCES: Leroy Stone, *Urban Development in Canada* **(1967); Statistics Canada.**

21

Managing the Regional Coalition Today

It fits with Walt's interpretation of events here, I think, that the single most striking feature of Canadian metropolitan growth over the past few decades has not been the rise of Toronto as the new Laurentian emperor of Canada, but the rise of far-western regional metropolitan centres in Calgary and Vancouver.

In the somewhat misleading shorthand customarily used for such purposes, "Toronto" no doubt does still more or less dominate the Canadian banking system. The Toronto Stock Exchange is still by far and away the largest of the Toronto, Montreal, Vancouver, and Alberta stock exchanges (and the one most often noticed outside Canada). Trucking in Ontario remains considerably more dependent on the Canadian national market than in either of Atlantic or western Canada.

And of course, again, the 1990 men in suits I overheard talking at the Wedgewood Hotel in Vancouver wouldn't still be getting into such arguments, if Toronto didn't still have great national influence. It is a recurrent complaint as well (even in Toronto, it sometimes seems) that Toronto is still too much of a one-sided headquarters for what there is of a national English-language media and communications system in Canada today.

Yet, as Walt himself puts it, "The deepest trend is that – like such places as Halifax, Montreal, Winnipeg, Calgary, and Vancouver – Toronto is becoming a *regional* metropolitan centre itself, in its own part of Canada, in North America, and in the world at large." Toronto has had intimate ties with New York City back to the seventeenth century. (As Harold Innis once so poetically explained, Walt notes, the "struggle waged between the Iroquois and the Hurons," which culminated in the 1640s, "was a prelude to the struggle between New York and Montreal, which dominated the economic history of Ontario.") Much more recently, the alleged new heir of the old Laurentian empire in Canada has been developing fresh commercial intimacies with such places as Atlanta and (as in the case of Vancouver) Los Angeles and Hong Kong – or even Santiago and Mexico City.

Ted's sketch of the coalition at work in 1993

Again, Ted argues that Canada-wide trucking statistics provide one rough handle on this more recent regionalization of the old Canadian east-west economic system, which the merchants of Montreal once did so much to pioneer. And even Walt agrees that, while the numbers for 1993 are somewhat ambiguous and already rather dated, they do have their own short story to tell.*

Ted's simplest cut at the data divides the country into four regions: Atlantic Canada, Ontario, Quebec, and western Canada. (For some purposes, Ted notes, BC and the Prairie provinces are separate regions. But in the most general case their domestic economies are intimately related, and in this same sense the northern territories fall in naturally with western Canada as well.)

A first point here is that (as of 1993) in *none* of these four regions do trucking revenues generated in the relevant rest of Canada exceed the revenues generated inside the region itself. Quebec comes very close, and Ontario is not too far behind. But in all regions of the country, the domestic regional market is more important than the Canadian national market.

If you do divide western Canada into separate BC and Prairie regions, then Atlantic Canada has the most apparently self-sufficient regional economy. But when you aggregate BC and the Prairies, western Canada becomes the most self-sufficient region by a considerable margin (and the one least dependent on the national market – or as the Quebec sovereigntist movement prefers to say, the Canadian economic space).

A host of complications in this very general picture inevitably arise when you start to look at the finer print. Manitoba and

---

* The numbers for 1993 were published in December 1995, and this was the last time that Ted (who claims to be quite busy in Ottawa) had a chance to ponder the subject in depth. Examples of some actual numbers appear in Exhibits 29 and 31. Ted has also sent along a short item on much broader "preliminary projections of the 1990 interprovincial and international trade flows" in Canada. These suggest that "shifts in trade flows from provincial to foreign markets were most prominent in Quebec and Alberta" in 1995, and that, in the same year, Ontario was "the only province to record an interprovincial surplus."

Prince Edward Island, for example, are both significantly more dependent on trucking revenues earned in Ontario than are other parts of their respective regions. Ontario and Quebec, Ted notes, depend on each other a great deal, and if they are combined into a single central Canadian region, this particular chunk of vast northern geography is almost as self-sufficient as western Canada. Ontario alone, on the other hand, is in fact somewhat more dependent on western Canada than it is on Quebec.

Finally, taking account at the same time of trucking movements between Canada and the United States complicates the general Canadian domestic picture yet again. Ontario is most dependent on trucking revenues earned in the US, followed closely by Quebec. Atlantic Canada is the one region where revenues earned in the US are (slightly) more important than revenues earned in the rest of the country. And western Canada is the region least dependent on US revenues. (In 1993 only some 12% of western Canada's total Canada-US trucking revenues came from the US, as opposed to 24% in Ontario.)

Western and Atlantic Canada
in the Canadian economic space

Ted's sketch here shows clearly enough how – as mere vestiges of a time when something like the Laurentian thesis was closer to the mainstream of Canadian economic development than it is now – Ontario and Quebec still are selling considerably more, comparatively, to the Canadian national market than either of Atlantic or western Canada. Ted also likes to stress, however, that even in Atlantic and western Canada, the national market continues to have some not altogether negligible significance.

If you treat the far western provinces of BC and Alberta together as a region, for instance, in 1993 just under 25% of all trucking revenues from Canadian shipments originating in BC and Alberta were earned in other parts of Canada. Just under 29% of these rest-of-Canada revenues for BC and Alberta were earned in Ontario, and another 17% came from Atlantic Canada and Quebec. At the other end of the country, about 26% of all trucking revenues from shipments originating in Atlantic Canada were earned in Quebec, Ontario, and western Canada.

This is the particular recent experience that Ted thinks some new form of Canadian national economic policy should build on. One key goal of this new policy would be to maximize the involvement in and benefits from the Canadian economic space in *every region* of the country. And this is important, Ted argues, both as a sort of economic safety net for Canadian national social policy, and even as a significant enough element in the wider relentless search for jobs, jobs, jobs.

On this view, Ted notes as well, Canada has, for the moment, probably come quite close to maximizing the job and related benefits it can get from the "transnational" global economy (with special reference to the global economic leader in the USA). Current efforts at international diversification in such places as the Asia Pacific region and Latin America may make a lot of sense. But even on the most optimistic scenario, it will take considerable time for these efforts even to start to pay off.

Thus reinvigorating the Canadian domestic national economy – which, according to World Bank statistics, is still one of the ten or fifteen largest national economies in the world today – has its own attractions as a job-creation strategy. Ted himself will even ask, in his more bold and confident moods: "How else are we finally going to attack the persistently too-high levels of unemployment we still have virtually all over Canada, short of dismantling our present social policy, and forcing a lot of people to work at poverty levels in jobs that don't need to be done,"?"

Of course, the new kind of national economic policy Ted has in mind couldn't be the same as John A. Macdonald's old National Policy of the later nineteenth century. For one thing, the new international trading regimes of the late twentieth century *have* virtually outlawed many of the characteristic strategies of these old kinds of national policies. And for another, the new policy would be explicitly designed to benefit western and Atlantic (and even northern) Canada, as much as Ontario and Quebec. Meeting these objectives, Ted concedes, would present some daunting challenges. But he he sees "no reason in principle why these challenges cannot be handled effectively, if that's what we in Canada really want to do."

Walt's counter-argument
on the death of the national business class

Walt says he would quite like to believe that Ted's new kind of national economic policy is possible. But (as Walt puts it himself), "It puts a lot of strain on my sense of economic realism."

Here Walt stresses again his view that to have a workable national economic policy you need a national business class. French-speaking Quebec, Walt says, is now the only part of Canada that comes at all close to meeting this requirement. And the nation in this case is not exactly Canada as we know it today.

In the rest of the country, the vast realignment from the empire of the St. Lawrence to the coalition of regional economies has meant that even the colonial imitation of a national business class Canada used to have is now, for all practical purposes, dead. Given the nature of the vastly realigned new Canadian economic system, no new national business class is likely to arise to replace the old one. And, in his worst moments at least, Walt thinks that this probably makes any quest for Ted's new kind of Canadian national economic policy futile at best.

As evidence, Walt submits the views of what he calls "so many contemporary English-speaking Canadian business leaders." Not too long ago, at his and Madeleine's house by the Ottawa River, he actually read some recent representative reflections of Canadian business leaders, from a book he had close at hand: "Everything is north-south ... Eighty percent of my executives want to be transferred to the U.S. ...It's not a matter of if Canada becomes part of the States, but when ... Canada is doomed, I think it is hopeless ... Canadian nationalism is nothing more than anti-Americanism, and you can't build a national pride or a nation on negatives like that ... We are not even pretending any more to have an armed force to defend Canada ... Canada should become part of the United States."*

---

*Walt's book here is Diane Francis, *Underground Nation*, 179, 183.

Ted's infinite faith in the people of Canada

Ted's first reaction to Walt's argument in this case is that there are many different people involved in business at all levels, in Canada and many other places. He agrees with Walt that the old national business class in Canada is virtually dead. But he says this may finally be quite a good thing. "It was always more British imperial than Canadian national in any case," he claims, "and it was certainly never very inspirational in the Maritimes or the west – or in French-speaking Quebec."

Ted also agrees that the present vastly realigned Canadian regional coalition is not likely to throw up some new national business class on the old model. And "the international trade agreements of the late twentieth century *are* to no small extent intended to inhibit this sort of development in any case." Under the new rules (to take just one example), the Canadian economic policy Ted has in mind would have to extend any benefits of "national treatment" it may offer domestic enterprises to firms outside Canada as well.

"Yet in the global economic order today," Ted likes to say (in his stronger moments), "there is no good reason that US or European or Asian or Latin American businesses can't help fulfil Canadian national policy objectives to strengthen Canada's east-west economic space, for their own international purposes. Canada's national economy does not belong to any business class anymore. Like the Canadian national geography, it belongs to the people of Canada. And nowadays I don't think you absolutely do need a national business class to have a national economic policy. All you need is a democratic people that is vital and energetic enough to look after itself."

It's at this juncture that Walt just smiles, politely: "But that's exactly the point, Ted. Politicians and bureaucrats like you aren't the democratic people. The democratic people are complicated and disorganized. How can they be vital and energetic enough to look after themselves? Most of us don't have the time, or the interest if we had the time. How can any sensible person have faith that something as vague and amorphous as the people of

Canada can manage some new national economic policy in their own interests? And besides" (and here Walt almost seems sad or wistful or troubled or even worried, or something like that): "who are the people of Canada, anyway? Where do they come from? Why are they here? Where are they going? What do they want to do? And, when you get right down to it, do they even exist?"

Exhibit 31
Canadian For-hire Trucking
in Canada and the United States, 1993

Region of Origin	Percentage of revenues earned in		
	Home region	Rest of Canada	United States
Atlantic Canada	57.9	20.6	**21.5**
Quebec	39.3	37.7	**23.0**
Ontario	41.3	34.9	**23.8**
Western Canada (& Yukon & Northwest Territories)	75.3	12.9	**11.8**

SOURCE: Statistics Canada.

Exhibit 32
Regional For-hire Trucking in Canada, 1993

*Percentage of revenues generated in home region
and other parts of Canada*

Originating in BC & Alberta		Originating in Ontario	
Rev generated in	Percentage	Rev generated in	Percentage
BC & Alberta	**75.5**	**Ontario**	**54.2**
Ontario	7.1	Quebec	17.0
Saskatchewan	5.9	BC & Alberta	14.8
Manitoba	4.3	Atl Provinces	8.6
Territories	3.1	Manitoba	3.4
Quebec	2.3	Saskatchewan	1.9
Atl Provinces	1.8	Territories	0.1
CANADA	100.0	CANADA	100.0

SOURCE: Statistics Canada.

Eight

WHO ARE THE PEOPLE OF CANADA, ANYWAY?

22

Geographic Descent

We were on the porch of Ted and Veronica's house in the Glebe district of Ottawa, just this past summer, when Walt posed his questions about how the people of Canada could manage their own national economic policy, and who they were in any case. It was a gorgeous day, and all six of us were on our way to another picnic in the Gatineau hills, in the hypocritical forest green minivan that Ted and Veronica like to drive around.

"Someone from California," Madeleine remarked, as we were getting into the minivan, "might say that there just aren't enough Canadian people to spend all that much time talking about." But then later, when we had finished our picnic, she raised the subject again. "Who are the people of Canada, anyway?" she said. "That's a good question. Why don't you men talk about it for a while, and we women will just listen." (And then she lay back on the grass to listen herself, in white shorts and a tight purple jersey, prompting me to reflect silently, in my own mind, that if the people of Canada included Madeleine, they must be worth talking about for at least a while.)

People and geography

In fact, neither my wife nor my sister are women who share Madeleine's enjoyment in listening to men talk. So Madeleine became an audience of one for the five of us. And even she would sometimes comment briefly on what we said.

To start with, Walt (who had raised the issue in the first place) pointed out that "in its most ancient political meaning, a 'people' were all related by what my grandmother used to call 'blood' – in the sense of 'blood is thicker than water.' And we can see the most ancient origins of this habit in North America if we look back just a few hundred years in our own history."

"In theory at least," Walt went on, "historic aboriginal political communities in Canada were typically defined as the biological descendants of some common ancestor. Your 'nation' in this sense was an extension of sorts of your family, with all the good and bad things that implies."

Some national political communities in various parts of the world, Veronica quickly pointed out, "still honour a version of this tradition." A "people" on this understanding involves all those belonging to a particular cultural or ethnic or racial group.

But we all agreed that, as in other parts of the new world, of course, the people of Canada today cannot possibly be defined in this way. "We" are, instead, a people defined by geographic rather than biological descent. And the people of Canada simply includes everyone who, for one reason or another, chooses to live within the boundaries of Canada's vast geography.

The virtues of geographic descent

My wife thought that there might be some advantages to this arrangement. Walt agreed. "The key point about government or the state," he said (in that way he has), "is that it claims a monopoly of legitimate force over a particular geographic territory. And geography probably is the purest substance around which a democratic people can take shape."

Veronica commented on how some today argue that in the age of global electronic communications geography has become an obsolete point of reference for "community building." Personally, she thought it was "marvellous that, as individuals, we can now choose to identify with all kinds of non-geographic communities around the world, over the Internet and so forth."

Then Ted pointed out that "the first and most fundamental purpose of government or the state is to preserve law and order, and I just don't see how you can do this over the Internet. It can only be done over geographic territory."

I said myself that I thought we were light years away from knowing how to do this for the territory of the entire planet Earth, without creating some abhorrent tyranny at the same time. My guess is that real freedom and democracy will only ever be practical possibilities at the level of the national state. A political organization that claimed a monopoly of legitimate force over the entire planet could only grow out of the barrel of a very big gun.

Exhibit 33
Voter Turnout in Canadian Federal Elections Since the Second World War

Election Year (& Winning PM)	% Eligible Voters Voting
1945 (Mackenzie King, L)	75
1949 (St. Laurent, L)	74
1953 (St. Laurent, L)	**68**
1957 (Diefenbaker, PC)*	74
1958 (Diefenbaker, PC)	**79**
1962 (Diefenbaker, PC)*	**79**
1963 (Pearson, L)*	**79**
1965 (Pearson, L)*	75
1968 (Trudeau, L)	76
1972 (Trudeau, L)*	77
1974 (Trudeau, L)	71
1979 (Clark, PC)*	76
1980 (Trudeau, L)	**69**
1984 (Mulroney, PC)	76
1988 (Mulroney, PC)	75
1993 (Chrétien, L)	70
1997 (Chrétien, L)	**67**

*Minority government.

SOURCES: Royal Commission on Electoral Reform and Party Financing, and Elections Canada.

23

The First Canadians

Madeleine's initial reaction was that all this is "just theory, so far." But "who are the people of Canada as actual people? That's where this subject starts to become strange, or is it tense, or insubstantial, or something like that."

Walt was still reluctant to get right down to this point. "As a practical matter," he said, "if democratic people who define themselves by geographic descent are going to make a real national state, the geography involved can't be just any geography. It has to have some unique meaning and significance, in the past, present, and future." Then he agreed altogether with Ted that "Canada's geography already has the historic legend of the multiracial fur trade, in northern North America."

Veronica remarked that, "from the standpoint of the conventional norms of the present-day consumer society in all of North America, the fur trade legend is at least slightly crazy, as well as romantic and wild." But Walt claimed that it was also "quite factual and down to earth (and not at all the same as the regionally divisive Laurentian thesis which, exactly whenever it became obsolete, is certainly obsolete now)."

Then Ted said that in the twentieth century, the real legend of the fur trade in Canada "has attracted the attention of quite a few down-to-earth and even one or two intellectually brilliant people." And it continues to bubble down in the Canadian underground today. Walt added that "if they are going to serve their purpose effectively, legends of geographic descent probably ought to be somewhat strange and exotic and even slightly crazy, as well as romantic and wild – like a western movie in the USA."

"The Indian, Inuit and Métis peoples of Canada"

At this juncture, my wife said that we still weren't talking about Madeleine's real question. And she guessed that the place to start here was the particular sentence from the conclusion to Harold Innis's classic fur trade book of 1930, that I like to talk about so much myself: "We have not yet realized that the Indian and his culture were fundamental to the growth of Canadian institutions."

Walt said that "well over half a century later, we have at least come somewhat closer to this realization than we used to be." And Veronica said it's "an optimistic sign that what section 35 of Trudeau's Constitution Act, 1982, calls 'the Indian, Inuit and Métis people of Canada' have also come to play a role in the constitutional debate on the future of Canada and Quebec."

I said that I thought we were all still confused about this issue (aboriginals and non-aboriginals alike). And I was still more than a little confused myself. But I felt I at least understood my own point of view better than I used to. And I felt the various debates of the 1980s and 1990s had made my own point of view somewhat better informed than it was in the 1970s.

My wife said I should elaborate a bit on this point of view (about which she has always been quite sceptical herself). I think she was just trying to show how much she has had to put up with in her marriage. But, probably because everyone else was tired of talking for a while, I was coaxed into carrying on.

Fallacies of "stolen continents"

To start with here, I said, such recent cultural creations as the book, *Stolen Continents* (by Ronald Wright, who lives in Canada as it happens), have in some quarters helped crystallize juvenile feelings that certain European people stole Canada and other parts of the new world from "the Indians." And this seems to me both an insult to the real Indian, Inuit, and Métis peoples of Canada's past, and an altogether wrong and absurd point of departure for any practical discussion about anyone's future.

For one thing, even a nodding acquaintance with the history of the world will show that until quite recently the human past, on one level, has been not too much more than a continuous story of various groups of people stealing land from various other groups of people, for one alleged good reason or another.

In some respects, I would agree, it is always useful to be reminded of the terrible truth about the human past (though, as books like *Stolen Continents* tend not to point out, this also includes such things as some appalling treatment of North American aboriginal peoples by other North American aboriginal peoples: there is, alas, no group of people in world history that has a monopoly on either good or evil).

Yet the ultimately decisive point today is that Canada *is* to no small extent a creation of the *aboriginal* transportation technology of the canoe and portage. The plainest truth about Canadian history is that the likes of the Micmac, and the Algonquin, and the Huron and Iroquois, and the Assiniboine, and the Plains Cree, and the Kootenay, and the Haida, and the Kwakiutl, and the Chipewyan, and the Nahani were far from dumb objects from which other people could steal land. Without their knowledge, skill, and active exertion, the founding of Canada would never have taken place. And I've heard it said that there are more Indian, Inuit, and Métis peoples of Canada today than there have ever been in the past.

Sovereigntist contagion

My second thought in this context was that the example of the late twentieth-century Quebec sovereigntist movement has been lamentably contagious in northern North America. Some current aboriginal political leaders argue that Canada's First Nations should constitute a separate sovereign nation, somehow analogous to the proposed new sovereign nation of Quebec (and likewise still somehow associated with Canada as well).

As I understand it, in the last few decades two potentially related practical concepts have arisen. The first is "aboriginal self-government" and the second is "Nunavut" – the soon-to-be third northern territory of Canada, created out of the more easterly parts of the present Northwest Territories.

The implementation of Nunavut is now underway. Beginning in 1999, a new popularly elected government will gradually assume control over the new territory. Inuit peoples of the Canadian Arctic constitute about 80% of the new territory's population, and in this and a number of other respects Nunavut (with a total population of about 22,000) might be characterized as a mild form of Inuit state within Canada. Yet as best as I can tell from the Internet, it will not be an Inuit sovereign nation or "national state." The circumstances of both the Inuit and the Arctic are also so unique, I would guess, as to make Nunavut an unlikely precedent for developments in other parts of the country.

Beyond the Inuit of the Arctic, there are, on the widest definition employed by Statistics Canada, somewhat more than a million aboriginal people of one sort or another in Canada today. If the Charlottetown Accord of 1992 had been implemented, at least a version of aboriginal self-government would have begun to take shape among many of these people. Alas, the referendum on the Accord suggested considerably less popular support for this concept among aboriginal people at large than among aboriginal political leaders. As best as I can make out, there is now some doubt about just how much support current aboriginal leaders command from anyone. And, for the moment, this has tended to dampen wider national interest in aboriginal issues in the continuing constitutional debate (though the recent election of Phil Fontaine as Assembly of First Nations "national chief" may mark a turn in fresh directions).

Going native in your own country

I concluded my monologue at the Gatineau picnic by saying that the aboriginal side of the constitutional debate over the past few decades has brought me to two rather vague but more or less resolute personal conclusions.

The first is that Canada ought to continue to make some kind of rapid practical progress on turning itself into a much better present home for the descendants of the first heroes of its real history (or anti-heroes, if you like, or heroines and all that).The second is that, in principle, the aboriginal peoples of Canada simply ought to be part of the people of Canada at large – the highly honoured first Canadians of today's democratic national state. Or, after some inner turmoil, I've concluded that I do not believe in any form of separate First Nations sovereignty.

I should quickly add that, as a practical matter, I think I can appreciate why many aboriginal people are still reluctant to see themselves as simply the first Canadians. And I feel this is ultimately the fault and the responsibility of the present non-aboriginal majority. If "we" want "them" to see themselves as one of "us," then we must first see ourselves as one of them.

The concept of geographic descent in this sense, I think, implies that when you choose to be part of the geographic people, you also choose to be a descendant of the first people who knew the geography. Thus all Canadians today are spiritual descendants of the Micmac, and the Algonquin, and the Huron and Iroquois, and the Assiniboine, and the Plains Cree, and the Kootenay, and the Haida, and the Kwakiutl, and the Chipewyan, and the Inuit of Nunavut, and on and on.

We are all, in other words, *natives* of the place in which we live now. (Or, if you like, we are all Indians now, and they have stolen our old-world souls.) This is the destiny we have chosen – either by coming here or by not going somewhere else. It puts us in touch with the ancient Great Spirit of the vast and rugged geography of northern North America, from coast to coast to coast. And it enriches our lives, which are too often trapped in the great banality of high technology. (And in yet another sense again, it is just a particular national way of recognizing the ultimate new universal truth of the global village: that in the very end, we all descend from the first human beings, and we are all just human beings together, today.)

Of course, all this is very ambitious and "long term." When I finished my monologue, my sister, Veronica, said my point of view was light years away from how virtually anyone thinks at the moment (non-aboriginal *or* aboriginal), and altogether unrealistic and absurd. My wife just looked smug and content. Ted and Walt smiled and said nothing. Then, when all of them had finished, Madeleine propped herself up on one of her gorgeous elbows and remarked: "Well I think that's quite an interesting idea." And, for the moment, that's good enough for me.

Exhibit 34
Total Population with Aboriginal Origins
Canada and Provinces and Territories, 1991

	Total Population with Aboriginal Origins	% Total Population of Province/Territory
Northwest Territories	35,390	61.6
Yukon Territory	6,385	23.1
Manitoba	116,200	10.8
Saskatchewan	96,580	9.9
Alberta	148,220	5.9
British Columbia	169,035	5.2
Nova Scotia	21,880	2.5
Ontario	243,555	2.4
Newfoundland	13,110	2.3
Quebec	137,615	2.0
New Brunswick	12,815	1.8
Prince Edward Island	1,880	1.5
CANADA	**1,002,670**	**3.7**

SOURCE: Statistics Canada.

Canadiens et Québécois

Another key element in the fur trade legend is that, though Canada has a long founding era, in which many different people were involved, it really has *no founding peoples*. And this is one part of the legend that makes it so conveniently inspirational for the increasingly culturally diverse country that looms on the horizon of the twenty-first century.

When we were discussing all this in the Gatineau hills, however, Veronica stressed that it does not imply denying some other equally plain truths about the Canadian past. Thus, just as the aboriginal peoples of Canada were the "first Canadians" (and Canada, itself, is an aboriginal word), the first people who actually called themselves Canadians – or, more exactly, les Canadiens – were the descendants of migrants from France who settled in the lower St. Lawrence valley of present-day Quebec, during the seventeenth and eighteenth centuries.

What does Quebec want?

Both these migrants and their descendants today, Veronica stressed as well, spoke and still speak French – as do smaller numbers of Canadians in all parts of the country (especially in the old colony of Acadia on the Atlantic coast, and in parts of the old Canadian "pays d'en haut" in present-day Ontario). That is why section 16 of the Constitution Act, 1982, declares that "English and French are the official languages of Canada."*

Of course, I couldn't help pointing out myself, this undeniably real aspect of the past, present, and future of the people of Canada is also what ultimately leads to the present-day sov-

---

*English and French are nowhere explicitly called "official languages" in the Constitution Act, 1867, which established the old British Dominion of Canada. But the 1867 Act does provide (in section 133) that either language may be used in the parliament of Canada and in federal courts, and that the records and acts of the Canadian federal parliament shall be published in both languages.

ereigntist movement in Quebec. However you look at it, it is the plain truth that the Canadian history of the past two and a half centuries has bequeathed two geographically concentrated linguistic majorities in Canada today – a French-speaking majority within the boundaries of the province of Quebec, and an English-speaking majority in the so-called rest of the country.

Even in the age of high technology, I went on, language in this sense is the key to communication, and communication in this sense is the key to any *democratic* political system. Even though the will of the majority is not the only principle of democracy, it is a necessary and crucial principle. And the majority in Quebec only speaks one language, and the majority in the rest of the country only speaks another language.

Considerations of this sort, Walt agreed, "lie at the bottom of the Quebec sovereigntist movement's highest and most convincing argument for the existence of not one but two democratic peoples, within the historic geographic unity of Canada today." Then Ted added that, after a generation of increasingly monotonous controversy and public debate, "it now ought to be clear what at least 60% of the francophone majority in Quebec wants" (or, as Veronica still insists on stressing, "wanted in October 1995"). It wants to be constitutionally or officially or legally or somehow or other enduringly and unalterably recognized as a democratic people in its own right.

The people of Quebec

Walt quickly picked up some of the more troubling issues here. It could be and often enough is argued that recognizing a separate democratic people of Quebec "implies reverting to an earlier (and less pure) approach to defining a democratic people, than the neutrally inclusive or globally universal principle of mere geographic descent." On the tightest version of this reading, to be an authentic part of the aspiring democratic "Québécois" you have to be a "pur laine" biological descendant of the original seventeenth- and eighteenth-century migrants from France.

Alternatively (Walt went on), a step or two away from this most ancient tradition, it is sometimes said that the Quebec sovereigntist movement's definition of a democratic people "substitutes the principle of language for geographic descent." A Québécois in this sense is someone whose mother tongue is French. And this can take in the likes of recent black migrants from such places as Haiti or Senegal, other migrants from such places as North Africa or Vietnam, and even still other migrants from France or Switzerland, or other parts of Canada itself.

At this point, Ted said that "there certainly are some old tribalist overtones in the Quebec sovereigntist movement today," and we all agreed. (How, to take just one recent example, can anyone who remembers the antics of Jacques Parizeau and Bernard Landry right after the 1995 referendum imagine otherwise?) Yet Walt pointed out that there are analogous overtones in English-speaking Canada and every other part of the world. And "while sentiments for and against such things can easily be mobilized for partisan purposes, it is quite mistaken to imagine that any kind of tribalism is essentially, or in principle, what the Quebec sovereigntist movement is all about.

"When Lucien Bouchard," Walt went on, "claims that the present geographic territory of Quebec is inviolable, he is pointing to the deepest truth about sovereigntist aspirations. The Quebec sovereigntist argument for two democratic peoples within the geographic unity of Canada is ultimately based on the same inclusive and open-ended principle of geographic descent as the rival argument for one united people of Canada at large."

Veronica would not agree to this. But Ted and my wife were more receptive, and I still think that Walt is absolutely right myself. Viewed in its most sympathetic light, the Quebec sovereigntist argument just draws attention to the theoretically secondary but still quite crucial problems of democratic communication, that the presence of two geographically concentrated linguistic majorities presents. And personally, I have reached the point where I'd be happy enough to see all of Canada face up to these problems head on, and get them out of the way.

As best as I can make out, at least, the decisive issue here isn't language by itself. It is the *geographic concentration of linguistic majorities.* If the current proportions of English and French-speaking Canadians were more or less evenly distributed geographically, from coast to coast to coast, then something like Pierre Trudeau's solution might make sense. Now that we have some extended practical experience with this issue, however, we ought to be able to see how, given the geographic distribution of the two language groups that does exist down on the ground, trying to define a single officially bilingual democratic people can only lead to a democratic national state in which the *majority of people* in *both groups* will justly tend to feel some never-ending sense of grievance and unfair treatment. (And, given the importance of the will of the majority in a democratic system, a democratic national state of this sort is likely to be congenitally turbulent and unstable – which is, more or less, exactly what Canada has been, ever since it started to become a real democratic national state in the 1960s.)

Another kind of argument

Veronica, of course, wanted to stress a different perspective on events. She is probably a more clever and intelligent person than I am, and I do agree that she has a few sharp countervailing points. All of them seem to me to reduce to another kind of argument, and you can get at it in a number of ways.

You can wisely observe, for instance (as Veronica has been telling me for years), that, especially in the age of high technology, the language communication problem in a geographic-descent democracy whose people speak more than one language is not absolute or infinite. Recent Canadian public life has become masterful in the art of simultaneous translation.

Here even my wife agrees that there are in fact quite large numbers of Canadian people, on both sides of the linguistic divide, who, while not seriously able to *speak* in the other tongue (especially to the satisfaction of the combative sovereigntist journalists who work for Radio-Canada in Quebec), nonetheless have some vague appreciation of and even affection for the cadences of both English and French.

At the Gatineau picnic, Ted also pointed out that, while French Canadians had more than their fair share of reasons to grieve in the old British Dominion of Canada, Georges Étienne

162

Cartier as well as John A. Macdonald was among its reputed founding fathers. Its first French-Canadian prime minister (Wilfrid Laurier) was elected as long ago as 1896, and its second ("Uncle" Louis St. Laurent) in 1949.

Laurier, Walt pointed out, was widely regarded in francophone Quebec as "un roi nègre." Madeleine herself jumped in here, to recall that one of Uncle Louis's grandsons (Gilles St. Laurent) even had the gall to run as a Quebec Reform Party candidate in the 1997 federal election. Then Walt briefly explained how Canada's third French-Canadian prime minister, Pierre Trudeau, "was more an heir of Laurier's French-Canadian nationalist rival, Henri Bourassa, than of Laurier himself." Yet, as Ted put it, "the rabid 1960s separatist Pierre Vallière's literary characterization of francophone Quebecers, as *Nègres blancs d'Amérique*, ought to be at least partly qualified, by the plain truth that, even today, the USA has yet to elect even its first Oreo-cookie black president."

All of *us*, in any case, agreed to this. And Walt went on to point out that "the very concept of a 'Québécois people' is historically anachronistic. As recently as the 1950s, according to Madeleine's French-Canadian grandmother, the term Québécois just meant a resident of Quebec City." Veronica stressed again that the modern French-speaking inhabitants of the lower St. Lawrence valley "*were* the first people to call themselves Canadians, and in the French-language primary historical sources they are known as Canadien not Québécois." And then Ted raised the most foolish but intriguing question: "If Quebec really does secede, will the name of the legendary Montréal Canadiens hockey team be changed to the Montréal Québécois?"

The people of Canada in Quebec

Walt of course reminded Veronica that both the old British Dominion of Canada and the old Roman Catholic Church in Quebec are now just historical memories. "Nothing anywhere is any longer the way it used to be. It is finally the rise of the new national democracy in Canada, with its English-speaking majority, that has spawned the sovereigntist movement among the French-speaking majority in Quebec. And time only moves backwards in books of science fiction."

After nodding quickly, however, Veronica continued to stress that some 40% of the Quebec francophone majority voted No in the 1995 referendum. And "yes, the numbers do suggest that quite a few sovereigntist voters stayed away from the polls in the federal election of 1997. But it must mean something that the Bloc Québécois only won some 38% of the popular vote in its latest democratic contest. Still more recent opinion polls suggest that only about the same percentage of Quebecers favour so-called sovereignty, all by itself."

I pointed out myself that there is a francophone majority in Quebec both in the sense that some 82% of the province's total population reports a French mother tongue, and in the sense that some 58% of all Quebecers today can only speak French. And it is a simple mathematical truth that if *all* the unilingual franco-phones in Quebec were to vote Yes in a sovereignty referendum, the sovereigntist movement would win by a quite clear majority. Yet this has still not happened – even though both the 1980 and 1995 referendum questions included references to some continu-ing association with the rest of Canada.

I think it is mistaken to exaggerate what all this implies about the prospects for the short-, mid-, or long-term future of "Canada and Quebec" today. And I think Veronica often does this. To me, her over-aggressive partisanship for what she calls "Canadian federalism" and "Canadian unity" blinds her to the plainest political truth about just how different French-speaking Quebec really is, and, no doubt, will always be.

But at the Gatineau picnic, we finally all agreed that, even among the present francophone majority in Quebec (let alone the majority of Quebec's total population), significant enough numbers of voters still do see themselves as, first and foremost, part of the democratic people of Canada at large.

I can't quite see how any event will erase this fact in any foreseeable future. It, too, is an undeniable reality in Canada today, with its own deep historical roots. And if someone actually were going to resolve the problem of Canada and Quebec, it, too, would have to be dealt with, in one way or another.

Exhibit 35
Variations in First Identity
Canadian Provinces and Regions, 1993

Province or Region	% Population Who Identify With*		
	Canada First	Canada and Province Equally	Province First
Quebec	**38**	**9**	**49**
Atlantic Canada	72	6	18
British Columbia	**60**	**23**	**13**
Prairies	**80**	**6**	**12**
Ontario	94	1	3

*"Neither" and "No Opinion" responses have been excluded.

SOURCE: Gallup Poll Canada.

25

The Long British Subjection
of the Anglo-American Frontier
in the True North, Strong and Free

In the end, Veronica and I were at opposite ends of the Gatineau-picnic spectrum on the people of Quebec and the people of Canada in Quebec. Madeleine, Ted, Walt, and my wife fell in between (with my wife closest to me). We finally all agreed with Ted that "there probably will have to be another Quebec referendum to settle this – if it's going to get settled at all."

Then Madeleine said: "Well, now it's time for British North America and all that." And we all agreed with this, too. Walt set the stage, again, with his historical expertise.

The legend of the founding fur trade in northern North America (as Walt put it) "also shows how there was an English-speaking presence within the geographic boundaries of what we call Canada today, long before la conquête in the middle of the eighteenth century."

Though so-called counterfactual arguments in history are always ultimately pointless, Walt went on, they can sometimes be mildly instructive. And, one might argue, "the history of the present Canadian territory in the seventeenth and earlier eighteenth centuries is such that, even if there had never been a conquest, Canada today would still be a place where a great many people speak English as well as French."

English-speaking peoples

Veronica, in her usual clever way, quickly saw how to exploit the direction in which Walt was moving. She argued that if there had been no conquest, Canada today would probably be a place with a French-speaking majority and an English-speaking minority, rather than the other way around. (But then Ted added, "Perhaps the coast-to-coast-to-coast English-speaking minority would even be a majority, within the geographic region of the old Hudson's

Bay Company, in the present-day Canadian west.")

In this sense, we all agreed again, la conquête *was* a decisive event. It determined that Canada today would have an English-speaking majority. Walt went on to say that it brought all of northern North America into the global British empire, "and (as the British historian G.M. Trevelyan wrote in the 1920s) set the stage for the nineteenth-century 'period in the settlement of Canada, Australia, and New Zealand which decided that those lands should be peopled mainly from Britain and should become parts of a free British Commonwealth of Nations.'"

At this point, my wife urged that there has been another massive English-speaking influence in the Canadian experience. And it, too, one might argue, would have had a dramatic and continuing impact, even without la conquête. (Here, Walt stressed, things do start to become quite complicated because la conquête in a number of respects set the stage for the American War of Independence, as well as the creation of the British Dominion of Canada some eighty-five or so years later: but we didn't want to try Madeleine's patience too much.)

Veronica summarized the crucial part of this last theme. She had just been reading in the paper about the Canadian-born American writer Bruce McCall. He says that crossing the border from the United States into Canada (outside Quebec) is just "a minor bureaucratic formality indicating that a single culture has merely shifted gears." Or nowadays, as Ted put it, "The United States not the United Kingdom is the great economic and cultural heartland of the English-speaking universe. And it is Canada's inescapable destiny, geographically and in almost every other way imaginable, to live right next door to the United States."

The anglo-American frontier in Canada

According to Walt, another way of approaching this inescapable destiny is to say that "Canada has been the northern edge of the anglo-American frontier in the USA – the place where the rampant culture of the new-world family farm and the American dream was blunted and then stopped dead, by the harsh and forbidding wilderness, further and further north."

Recalling some earlier thoughts from Walt, I noted myself that the traditional Canadian method for acknowledging this side of the story has been to talk quickly about the loyalist migrations of the late eighteenth century, in the wake of the War of Independence. Yet, as Ted reminded us all again, the fabled coming of the loyalists was only one of several earlier and later American frontier incursions into the harsh fur-trade wilderness, from the neutral Yankees of Nova Scotia to the covered-wagon continental vagabonds of the Canadian last best west.

Walt launched into his own mini-monologue here: "As the career of Sitting Bull and a host of Vietnam War draft resisters suggest, Canada in this sense has been both a destination and a safety-valve for the excesses of the American frontier. And as the likes of John Candy, Jim Carey, Michael J. Fox, Wayne Gretzky, Walter Houston, Norman Jewison, Guy Lombardo, Raymond Massey, Joni Mitchell, Anne Murray, Mike Myers, Mary Pickford, Martin Short, and Shania Twain testify, there certainly is a single anglo North American culture, of which Canadians have been ardent producers as well as consumers."

I remarked that there is also some room for vaguely comedic cultural confusion in all this. Judging from my television set, some American media figures (Jay Leno immediately comes to mind) tend to see Canada as a new-world Scotland to the England of the USA. And then Veronica said that Jay Leno was "not the only person I've seen on Hollywood TV who seems to believe that real people in Canada speak English with a Scottish accent."

British North America

Imagining that English-speaking Canadians talk with Scottish accents, Ted argued, "may at least be a sloppy Hollywood shorthand for the truth that there *is* some shifting of gears when you cross the border from the US into English-speaking Canada. And the old loyalist mythologies themselves have been another sloppy shorthand for the truth that this does have a lot to do with the extended history of the British empire in northern North America." In the same vein, Walt suggested, "Americans" abandoned the empire in the late eighteenth century. "Canadians" hung on for another two hundred years: they are, as Walt put it, "Americans who remained British subjects until 1947 (or, to be very exact, even until the middle of the 1970s)."[*]

Walt had now picked up Ted's theme, and inevitably he carried on (and on, and on). The legacies of the British empire in Canada have several dimensions. And one of them does involve large numbers of migrants to the country from the United Kingdom in the nineteenth and earlier twentieth centuries (as well as smaller numbers in the seventeenth and eighteenth, and even later twentieth centuries, right down to the present). From 1867 until the Second World War, the majority of people in the Dominion of Canada reported one or another form of British descent: English, Irish, Scottish, Welsh, and all that.

In terms of English-speaking accents and habits of mind, British origins in this respect seldom lasted beyond the initial migrating generation – as is still true today in the case of migrants from many other places. The Canadian-born children of British immigrants quickly became anglo-Americans, indistinguishable in many respects from citizens of the USA.

Unlike the United States, however, Canada remained a place where public and even some aspects of private life continued to be shaped by British institutions and the global English-speaking culture of the British empire, well into the middle of the twentieth century. Just before the First World War, the French political writer, André Siegfried, explained how Canadian politics was a story about "American actors on an English stage." And in various ways this is still true enough, even today.

British-style government and politics – on what now tends to be called "the Westminster model" – was just the most obvious aspect of British institutions in the old Dominion of Canada. Even after the First World War, Canadian higher education outside

---

[*]Just to review Walt's own understanding here, as discussed in various earlier footnotes and whatnot, from 1867 until the Citizenship Act of 1947, inhabitants of Canada were merely British subjects (though, as of 1921, they could also refer to themselves as Canadian Nationals when travelling abroad). Between the Citizenship Act of 1947 and the Citizenship Act of 1977 they were *both* British subjects *and* Canadian citizens. Since 1977 they have simply been Canadian citizens. If this is wrong, Walt wishes someone in Ottawa would let him know.

French-speaking Quebec, like the Canadian military establishment, was dominated by British precedents, and often enough even by personnel from the United Kingdom. (It was not until 1937, Walt pointed out, that the fur-trade guru, Harold Innis, became the first Canadian-born chairman of the old department of political economy at the University of Toronto.)

British institutions in a still broader sense have had a more diffuse impact on the people of Canada in the twentieth century. British movies at Odeon theatres were a part of Walt's Canadian childhood in the 1950s. And in the early 1960s, the American literary critic, Edmund Wilson, noted that "in spite of much Americanization" Canadian life still preserved "a British tradition of good order and capable handling." (It is amazing how Walt remembers these quotations so exactly, word for word – or maybe they aren't exactly word for word.)

Imperial echoes among the people of Canada today

At this stage of the debate, I couldn't help remarking myself that all of this has been much further from the surface of life for my three Canadian sons, who have happily grown up under the maple leaf flag, in the 1970s, 1980s, and 1990s. The majority of people in Canada have not reported British ethnic origins for some half a century now. The British empire has faded into the past, and the current "free Commonwealth of Nations" is just an obscure international organization, that you may or may not very occasionally read about in Canadian newspapers.

Ted agreed. In the age of Bill Clinton and Tony Blair, at the edge of the twenty-first century, "when you fly from the United States to the United Kingdom itself you are just shifting gears within a single culture." The shift is still more pronounced than when you move from the US to Canada: people in the United Kingdom do talk with one or another form of British accent (and, as in Australia, they drive on the wrong side of the road). Yet, as Walt added, in his characteristic style, "The notion of English-speaking Canada as some halfway house between Great Britain and the United States makes a lot less sense now, than it did when the cultural distance between the US and the UK was much greater than it is today. And it perhaps never did make at all as much sense as some people liked to pretend."

Even so, I couldn't resist adding, for my sister Veronica's benefit, that I supposed I would ultimately agree with my brother (who so likes to disagree with Veronica). Even today, much of what is conventionally said about how the people of Canada subtly differ from the people of the United States still has a lot to do with our historic over-extended apprenticeship, at the feet of the masters of the British empire.

Veronica looked at me as if I'd just revealed some dark family secret. But I pressed on.

When we still say, rightly or wrongly, that we are more polite and reserved, more law-abiding, less violent and more determined to live in safer towns and even big cities, more urbane and civil, less ideological and more tolerant, and (echoing an obscure passage in the Constitution Act, 1867) more concerned with "peace, order, and good government" than with "life, liberty, and the pursuit of happiness," we are still just remembering the lessons that our former British imperial masters tried to teach us.

Even in a new country in the new world, even a mere few hundred years of history does not disappear overnight. This, too, is a part of the legend of the fur trade in Canada. And, now that I have survived for more than half a century, I have begun to appreciate that, in a few minor respects, it may not be altogether a bad thing – even in the newest democratic national state.

Exhibit 36
Ethnic Origin, Canada, 1991

Group	% Population in Group
Multiple origins	28.9
French origins	22.8
British origins	20.8
European origins	15.4
Asian and African origins	6.0
Canadian and other origins	2.9
Aboriginal origins	1.7
Black origins	0.8
Caribbean origins	0.4
Latin, Central, and South American origins	0.3
Pacific Islands origins	0.0
ALL ORIGINS	100.0

SOURCE: Statistics Canada.

26

The More and More Mixed Community
of the Past, Present, and Future

I had barely managed to finish the last sentence of my remarks on the lessons our former British imperial masters tried to teach us when Walt jumped in with another of his weighty thoughts.

"The French and then the British empires in the new world," he began, "brought the French and English languages to Canada. And the British empire determined that Canada as we know it today has an English-*speaking* majority. But of course this does not imply that the people of Canada – inside or outside the boundaries of the province of Quebec – have been historically defined by some British or English or anglo cultural or ethnic majority (whatever that may or may not mean, exactly)."

Ted, who has an unmistakably non-anglo last name, quickly seconded Walt's new motion here. "It's at this point," he said, "that the founding legend of the fur trade in Canada projects its most potentially attractive image of the future. And in this respect, the story of the multiculturalism or cultural diversity that is so plainly evident on the streets of such places as Vancouver and Toronto today doesn't just reach back to the 1960s. It goes all the way back to Canada's long founding era, in the sixteenth, seventeenth, and eighteenth centuries."

Naturally, Walt agreed. The people who took the fur trade in northern North America all the way from the Atlantic, to the Arctic, to the Pacific oceans – and in the process created the historic geographic unity of Canada today – weren't just Aboriginal or French or English or any other one thing. They were an exotic mixture of Aboriginal and European and Other peoples, and they lived in a mixed society of what some recent writers have taken to calling "the middle ground." The mixed society of the fur trade blended a great variety of cultural habits and assumptions and made them all work together (more or less). And this original Canadian mixed society is the real historical ancestor of the Canada of the twenty-first century and beyond, that we can so obviously see arising not just on the streets of Vancouver and Toronto today, but on the streets of such places as Kitchener and Calgary and Victoria and Edmonton and Winnipeg and even Montreal, as well.

Over the rainbow

Veronica pointed out that there are senses in which this view of the world is "only slightly less crazy" than my view of how all Canadians are descendants of the Micmac and the Iroquois and the Cree and the Haida and so forth. She even argued that "most in the country still talk as if there were four *essentially separate* broad cultural communities among the people of Canada today – the aboriginal community, the French community, the English community, and the so-called multicultural community."

My own argument here was that, if you listen to the most authentic chords of the fur trade legend, this is just not what Canada's real founding era implies about the long-term Canadian future. And this time, Walt supported me.

By the late eighteenth century, Walt explained, when the fur traders of the North West Company had finally taken Canada from the Atlantic, to the Arctic, to the Pacific oceans, there were a few restricted clusters of people whose ancestors had earlier migrated from France, in the St. Lawrence valley and on the Atlantic coast. And, on the Atlantic coast, in the St. Lawrence valley, and in a few places immediately north of the Great Lakes, there were somewhat smaller numbers of people whose ancestors had originally migrated from various parts of the British Isles (often having first stopped over for several generations, as it were, in the British Thirteen Colonies of America).

At this point, however (Walt went on), the human community in the great bulk of the present Canadian territory was neither strictly "European," nor strictly "Indian," nor strictly anything else. It was an exotic mixture of old and new worlds. And it was the multiracial fur trade in this sense that pioneered a uniquely Canadian frontier in northern North America, and first created the historic geographic unity that acquired its first modern political expression in the Canadian confederation of 1867.

Walt noted as well that Henri Joly de Lotbinière, "one of the unfortunately less-remembered Canadian political characters from the age of John A. Macdonald (and Georges Étienne Cartier – and Wilfrid Laurier)," was a particularly intriguing figure in this respect. His political career began in 1861, and he would subsequently serve as premier of Quebec (1878–79), as Laurier's federal controller of inland revenue (1896–1900), and finally as lieutenant governor of British Columbia (1900–06).

In the original confederation debates of 1865, Joly de Lotbinière (showing some remarkable prescience, Walt argued, about the kind of Canada you can still see on the streets of such places as Vancouver and Toronto today), proposed "the adoption of the rainbow as our emblem. By the endless variety of its tints the rainbow will give an excellent idea of the diversity of races, religions, sentiments and interests of the different parts of the Confederation ... An emblem we must have, for every great empire has one; let us adopt the rainbow."[*]

Racial realism

My sister, Veronica, continued to argue (as she has argued with me for years now) that it is all too easy to sentimentalize and over-romanticize the founding fur trade era of the Canadian past. And, again, I almost always feel that I have to concede she has at least a few sharp and compelling arguments.

The "European side of the fur trade in Canada," she quite rightly pointed out, "almost systematically spread a wilderness culture of alcoholism among the country's aboriginal peoples, with some tragic long-term consequences." Some traders of European descent have left us journals and other written documents that convey their enthusiasm and respect for the habits of their aboriginal customers and co-workers. The writings of others "exude an unmistakable racist contempt, that was at best opportunistically concealed in face-to-face transactions."

Inevitably, Veronica pointed out as well that white male

---

[*]Quoted in Frank H. Underhill, *In Search of Canadian Liberalism* (Toronto: Macmillan of Canada, 1960), ii.

traders who remained in the hinterland for long periods often took Indian wives, "à la façon du pays." Some revelled in what Sylvia Van Kirk (drawing on documentary sources) has called the "many tender ties" of their Métis families, and saw their "country marriages" through to the ends of their lives. Others callously exploited their wives sexually and then moved on.

From another angle again, Walt conceded himself, "the Bank of Montreal was founded on profits from the fur trade, and made a number of white fur traders very rich. Nothing at all comparable would ever happen to the Indian and Métis peoples of Canada. And that is one key reason why there is still an aboriginal issue in the debate on the future of Canada and Quebec today."

In a similar way, I felt obliged to concede myself, some excessively smug Canadians used to think that the wider story of cultural diversity in the northern half of North America was more benign than in the neighbouring USA. There are even some odd intimations of this sort in the conclusion to Harold Innis's classic book of 1930, which attributes perhaps a few too many Canadian blessings to a northern fur trade that had no altogether exact analogues in the warmer regions further south.

In fact, for example, there were a few more people of African descent in early Canadian history than it was once customary to pretend. And, while never quite liable to the appallingly harsh fate of the "strange fruit hangin' from the poplar trees," in Billie Holiday's desperately haunting lament on black life in other parts of the new world, they seldom found much of a happy home in the true north, strong and free.

Ted added that Chinese labourers helped build the Canadian Pacific Railway in the late nineteenth century. But when they finished their work, they were rewarded with hostile restrictions and eventually outright prohibitions on Asian immigration to the first self-governing dominion of the British empire, down to the end of the Second World War.

Cultural diversity in Canada today

At the same time, again, Walt stressed that "the truth about human experience almost always has more than one side." And

"Henri Joly de Lotbinière did mean something when he talked about 'the diversity of races, religions, sentiments and interests of the different parts of the Confederation' in 1865."

Ted picked up this theme quickly. The initial mixing of various Aboriginals and various Europeans and various Others in northern North America would "set precedents for an increasingly realized wider diversity." Even before the nineteenth century, there were migrants who traced their descent to European places outside France and the United Kingdom. As Preston Manning so likes to point out, in the late nineteenth and earlier twentieth centuries the prairies of the Canadian west attracted large-scale migration from the steppes of eastern Europe, and (in Ted's words) "became the site of the new British Dominion of Canada's most vigorous early experiment in what would later be called multiculturalism."

Walt carried on. By the early twentieth century, the rapidly growing urban areas of central Canada had also begun to attract more diverse European migrations. After the Second World War, the restrictions on Asian migration were lifted. By the 1960s, various parts of Canada had begun to attract increasing numbers of migrants of African descent, especially from the old British West Indies (and eventually from the USA). By the middle of the 1980s, the top ten countries of origin for new migrants to Canada were Vietnam, Hong Kong, the United States, India, England, Poland, the Philippines, Jamaica, Guyana, and China.

In 1991 recent migrants accounted for some 38% of the population in the Toronto metropolitan region, 30% in Vancouver, 20% in Calgary, 18% in Winnipeg, 17% in Montreal, and 15% in the national capital region of Ottawa-Hull.

The future of the people of Canada

In 1991 as well, the single-largest group of all Canadians (some 29% in Canada at large, and 36% in Canada outside Quebec) reported their ethnic background as one or another combination of so-called "multiple origins." And despite noisy forces that still push in other directions, I noted myself, this last statistic also strikes me as something that points to a more and more crucial wave of whatever Canadian future there may or may not be.

At the edge of the twenty-first century, it is not just the people of Canada, collectively, but increasingly *individual Canadians*, who report one form or another of mixed descent. (Or, put another way, the Métis heritage of the fur trade era has taken a bold new lease on life.) And I think this ultimately can't help but bring increasing democratic social pressure to bear against all manner of conceptions of separate group rights.

Both Walt and Ted agreed with this – and it was clear enough that all three women believed something at least vaguely similar. "It is at least increasingly less of an exaggeration" (as Walt put it) "to say that the people of Canada trace their origins to more and more complicated combinations of places, in virtually all parts of the globe." The more this trend continues, the more unrealistic it will become to divide the national political community into a few broad groups. It may not be quite true yet to say that we are *all* multicultural now. But "surely this is the only workable logic of the direction in which we are moving."

On this same logic, and setting aside the strictly linguistic-majority issue for the moment, surely the only long-term cultural identity any of us can aspire to, as democratic citizens, must flow from our shared geographic descent. "This is both the most realistic future that confronts the people of Canada today," Walt said, "and the ultimate wisdom of the multiracial fur trade legend that defines the most authentic apprehension of a Canadian past." (And, Madeleine herself finally added, to sum everything up: "If this still seems an all-too-hopelessly vague and open-ended national vision, that is only because it still gives us lots of room, as individuals, to choose just what we want to be ourselves.")

Nine

LET'S JUST DO IT AND GET IT OVER WITH
(An immodest proposal)

Exhibit 37
The World's Fifteen Largest National Economies
1994

Standard Measure GNP (Billions US $)		Purchasing Power Parity* GNP (Billions Int'l $)	
United States	6,737	United States	6,737
Japan	4,321	China	2,989
Germany	2,075	Japan	2,664
France	1,355	Germany	1,614
Italy	1,101	India	1,179
United Kingdom	1,069	France	1,144
China	630	Italy	1,064
CANADA	**570**	United Kingdom	1,055
Brazil	536	Brazil	896
Spain	525	Russian Federation	780
Russian Federation	392	Indonesia	701
Mexico	369	Mexico	648
South Korea	366	**CANADA**	**621**
Netherlands	338	Spain	555
Australia	321	South Korea	470

*Purchasing power parity is defined as the number of units of a country's currency required to buy the same amounts of goods and services in the domestic market as one dollar would buy in the United States.

SOURCE: *The World Bank Atlas 1996.*

27

Can Quebec Secede?

We had almost finished our Gatineau picnic conversation on the people of Canada, when Walt said that he still didn't think we had even addressed, let alone answered, *his* first question. Could the kind of people of Canada we were all, in one way or another, pointing towards, actually create and manage some new national economic policy in their own interests?

Then Ted said that the more obvious immediate question was: "What happens if Lucien Bouchard and the PQ win the next Quebec provincial election, and hold another referendum, and the Yes side wins?" Before they tried anything else, Ted went on, the people of Canada somehow had to resolve the impossibly confused future of Canada and Quebec.

Rising to the height of the occasion at last (more or less)

Veronica of course objected that Lucien Bouchard may not win the next Quebec election. Or he may win the election, and cunningly decide not to hold another referendum. Naturally, Ted agreed. But he said he still thought that if "we just had a clear enough idea of how we'd deal with a Yes victory in a next referendum," then everything else would start to fall into place – including his new kind of "national economic policy that worked for everyone, from coast to coast to coast."

At this point, I foolishly said that I thought a lot of people in Canada outside Quebec had at least certain inklings, as it were, about how to resolve the impossible confusion, by more or less giving the francophone majority in Quebec what it seems to have said it wanted in 1995 – a sovereignty-association deal that works as well for the rest of the country as it does for Quebec.

I was surprised when I said this myself. And I was even more surprised that I suddenly had a faint glimmering of how my own case of confusion might turn into some form of workable future. Walt and Veronica, my wife, and even Madeleine just smiled. Ted said, however (I'm not sure just how seriously), that what I should do is write down something a little more like the details of what I had in mind, and send it to him.

In fact, it's taken me quite a while to do this. I'm still not sure yet whether I'm going to send it on to Ted. I'm not convinced that he would read it, and I can almost hear Veronica saying that it would be a waste of his time.

In any case, what I finally have managed to write on this ultimate subject might make a sensible enough conclusion to the reflections I've been jotting down here – about my personal voyage of discovery on the long, tortuous waterway of Canada and Quebec, since I first hitched-hiked with my high-school friends to the Gaspé coast, in the summer of 1963.

I should perhaps add up front that this conclusion comes in two installments. The first, here in Part Nine of my reflections, gives a rough sketch of the what I think might be the best solution: again, a new sovereignty-association deal that works as well for the rest of the country as it does for Quebec. The second installment, in Part Ten at the very end, suggests a few related things about the practical politics of the current *neverendum* debate, and about some of what seem to me the least happy alternatives to the kind of new deal that I think more than a few people of Canada actually do have rather dimly in mind.

Would Quebec unilaterally declare independence?

To start with, probably the worst that could happen if the Yes side won a next Quebec referendum, I'm assuming almost all of us would agree, is that Quebec would unilaterally declare independence, fracture the historic geographic unity of the northern fur trade, and leave the rest of Canada in limbo. And we do know that Jacques Parizeau entertained some such prospect in 1995 – encouraged, apparently, by an advisor in France.

Lucien Bouchard, on the other hand, was a Canadian federal cabinet minister in an earlier incarnation. He is supposedly more interested than Parizeau in some new partnership between a new sovereign Quebec and the rest of Canada.

Yet again, even in the 1995 referendum the Parti Québécois

position was that if the Yes side won, the present provincial government of Quebec would *try* to negotiate some new partnership (though exactly with whom or what has never been clear). But Quebec *would* unilaterally declare independence if this negotiation did not succeed – or more exactly, perhaps, if Quebec could not get the kind of deal it wanted from the rest of us.

As best as I can make out, this is still how Lucien Bouchard is thinking. Put another way, the official position of the present sovereigntist leadership is that if the only way of achieving recognition of a sovereign French-speaking people of Quebec, who put Quebec (not Canada) first, is ultimately to secede from the Canadian confederation, then that is what Quebec will do.

I should say, right up front, that I personally take this position quite seriously. If you examine the 1995 referendum question, and the accompanying public debate, I also think it's fair to say that in October 1995 the position was democratically endorsed not just by very close to 50% of Quebec's total population, but by some 60% of the francophone majority as well.

I don't myself think that the results of the June 1997 federal election dramatically qualify the significance of this endorsement. And, though there was an apparent resurgence of sentiment for so-called "renewed federalism" in Quebec by the fall of 1997, my own feeling is that, as on so many occasions in the past, this will probably once again prove to be so much grasping at straws.

Secession as a practical issue

Having said all this, I'd also agree that it's one thing to take what people say seriously, and another to believe that they can bring it off. In fact, as a practical matter, it seems to me rather unlikely that the Parti Québécois could successfully take Quebec out of Canada by some *unilateral* declaration of independence – even if the Yes side did win another referendum in the near future.

The crux of the issue here is that the sovereigntist option just does not have enough popular support, inside Quebec itself, to make any workable unilateral declaration of independence a realistic prospect. And this is ultimately because, as Veronica so likes to stress, there still are significant numbers of even French-speaking Quebecers who do put Canada (not Quebec) first.

To work through the argument quickly, ever since the build-up to the first referendum in 1980, the PQ has made it clear that the citizens of a sovereign Quebec would only pay taxes to the government of Quebec. This implies that any workable unilateral declaration of sovereignty or independence would have to be accompanied both by the mass resignation of Quebec's present members of the federal parliament, and by some strong mass consensus, among virtually all Quebec residents, to stop paying tax bills sent by the government in Ottawa.

Bringing this off would require a great bulkhead of democratic social pressure, to persuade reluctant Quebec taxpayers and members of the federal parliament (including several prominent cabinet ministers and probably the prime minister of Canada himself) to do what the sovereigntist movement wants. Generating this degree of pressure would require a decisively strong and convincing margin of victory on the Yes side. For the sake of argument, say, at least 60% of *the total Quebec population* would have to vote Yes, and perhaps considerably more. And there is virtually nothing in the current state of Quebec opinion, as far as I can see, to suggest that a Yes-side victory of anything like this magnitude is practically possible.

The sovereigntist movement's approach to this conundrum is to advance one or another form of the argument that if a mere 52% Yes vote was enough to bring Newfoundland into Canada in 1949, it also ought to be enough to take Quebec out a half-century later. Meanwhile, the federal government is asking the Supreme Court of Canada to rule on whether any Canadian province can legally secede from the present confederation.

Both these approaches finally seem to me disingenuous and beside the point. Even Jean Chrétien has conceded that if a *large enough* number of Quebecers democratically choose to secede from Canada, then the opinions of the lawyers who sit on the Supreme Court are irrelevant. On the other hand, even if 52% of the total population of Quebec were to vote Yes in a next referendum, that would still *not be enough, practically,* to prompt appropriate action by all the Quebecers whose democratic cooperation would be required, to bring off a *unilateral* declaration of sovereignty or independence successfully. (And this would be especially true if the referendum question included some reference to a future partnership with the rest of Canada – as, one can only assume, it almost certainly would.)

The unreal prospect of armed force

Quebec sovereigntists often argue that all this unfairly sets the democratic bar for the achievement of sovereignty too high. And, as best as I can tell from my bookshelves, there probably are more than a few historical examples of independence movements that have created new national states, with less-popular support than the Quebec sovereigntist movement enjoys right now.

Yet no one in particular is actually setting the bar this high. As Ted himself likes to argue, what has made the difference in other historical cases is that the political movement which claims to speak for the people of the aspiring new sovereign state has used armed force to press its claims. Reluctant new citizens, whose cooperation has been required to make a *unilateral* declaration of independence work, have ultimately been persuaded not by democratic social pressure, but by some credible anticipation that, if necessary, the aspiring new state's prospective monopoly of legitimate force will be vigorously applied.

I've noticed recently how, if you broach this branch of the subject over drinks in a bar, there are somewhat surprising numbers of people (well, men, in fact) who will say, yes indeed, the debate about the future of Canada and Quebec just might get down to some violent civil war. But my own experience has been that this feeling surfaces after just a few drinks, when the company's latent bellicosity stirs. Then it fades quickly after a few more drinks, when everyone starts to tell the truth.

It would not be all that surprising, I'd agree, if there were some random bouts of political violence in the wake of yet another sovereignty referendum in Quebec – of the sort that arose at Oka after the failure of the Meech Lake Accord, or even of the sort that the FLQ made infamous in the 1960s and early 1970s.

René Lévesque, however, founded the Parti Québécois in order to lead the Quebec sovereigntist movement in a more democratic direction. Personally, I would be surprised to see a PQ government of Quebec call out the Sûreté – or, as one friend of mine once jocularly suggested, the "Van Doos" – to compel reluctant residents of Westmount (or Outremont) to stop paying taxes to Ottawa. For one thing, this would only compel the federal government, which does command some more or less serviceable armed forces, to protect Canadian citizens in Quebec. And this certainly would lead to some form of actual civil war.

I don't think it's naive to suggest that there are just no *significant* numbers of people today, in either Quebec or the rest of the country, who are interested in deciding the political future of northern North America in a violent civil war. Some will say that is one of the problems with Canada (and Quebec). My own view is that this is one of the problems we don't have. (And I don't exactly mean this in any high moral sense: one likely enough outcome of a violent Canadian civil war is that all of Canada *and* Quebec, from coast to coast to coast, would ultimately just be annexed by the armed forces of the USA.)

Jean Charest's black hole

Of course, again, it may well be that only the most misty partisans of the Quebec sovereigntist movement have ever seriously imagined that Quebec would or could declare its independence from Canada altogether *unilaterally*. The prospect of unilateral secession has only ever been a threat (a "knife held to the throat," in the provocative imagery expounded a few years back by the late Quebec intellectual, Leon Dion), designed to pressure the rest of Canada into giving Quebec the kind of new deal it wants.

I feel there is more than a little to this myself. And I think it's fair enough for the rest of us, in our own national interests, to call the sovereigntists' bluff. At least until the opinion polls start showing 60% or 65% or 70% levels of support for the sovereigntist option in Quebec – among all Quebecers – we probably don't need to worry much about the prospect that Quebec will secede from Canada unilaterally, and leave the rest of us in limbo.

Alas, this does not at all mean that we don't *really* need to worry, period. And here I think the most relevant imagery has been provided by the current federal Progressive Conservative leader from Quebec, Jean Charest, in his one genuinely useful contribution to the 1997 federal election campaign.

Even allowing for assorted subtle adjustments in the Canadian political climate since the 1997 federal election, for instance, it certainly remains a likely enough prospect that there will be another Quebec sovereignty referendum in the not-too-distant future. And I think it is equally quite possible that the Yes side just could win this referendum, by something in the order of 52% (which *is* all it took to bring Newfoundland into Canada in 1949). And even though this would not be enough for Quebec to secede from Canada unilaterally, it would be more than enough to throw all of us, everywhere in Canada, into what Jean Charest has very aptly termed "a black hole."

The need to get out of the black hole as quickly as possible

The point about a black hole of this sort is that absolutely no one knows or can know what is inside it or where it may lead. It could even be that it is simply a state of oblivion from which the only practical escape is death. And, as best as I can make out, it is certainly true that no one in any part of Canada *really* does *know* what would happen if the Yes side won a next Quebec sovereignty referendum, by something in the order of 52%.

The PQ might say that it would try to negotiate a new partnership with the rest of the country. But there is no existing political organization that represents the rest of the country or Canada without Quebec, and in principle it is not at all clear just who or what the PQ ought to negotiate with in such a circumstance. On the other hand, as I've already discussed, even if the PQ tried to clear the air by unilaterally declaring the independence of Quebec, all this would do is add to the confusion.

On the other hand again, there would, nonetheless, be a strong perception that Canada was no longer what it had been the day before the referendum. There would be a vast uncertainty about what Canada might become in the future, and this would have rocky implications for financial markets in all parts of the country. Everyone with savings and investments in Canadian dollars – or even just a small piece of Canadian real estate, or an interest in the Canadian social safety net (even with all the new holes that all levels of government have lately been putting into the net's most tightly woven mesh) – would, rightly enough, feel suddenly and deeply insecure, and on, and on, and on. However you look at it, everyone in all parts of Canada would be in the black whole together, and we'd suddenly *all* have an interest in getting out of it *as quickly as we could.*

The Quebec sovereigntist movement, as best as I can make out, feels confident that the Quebec of its dreams would at least emerge from all this confusion better off than it is now. And for all I know, this may even be true. My concern is with the rest of the country, because that's where I live myself. If, as many among us *are* quietly coming to recognize, I think, *we* want to have any practical hope of surviving some likely enough journey into a black hole of this sort, more or less intact, we ought to be figuring out just how we would deal with a Yes victory in some next Quebec sovereignty referendum, right now.

Exhibit 38
National States with Population Sizes Comparable to Quebec and the Rest of Canada, 1994

Population (000s)			
Quebec	**7,281**	**Rest of Canada**	**21,966**
Norway	4,318	Netherlands	15,391
Finland	5,083	Saudi Arabia	17,498
Denmark	5,173	Australia	17,841
Isracl	5,420	Sri Lanka	18,125
Haiti	7,035	Malaysia	19,498
Switzerland	7,127	Iraq	19,951
Bolivia	7,237	Nepal	21,360
Austria	7,915	Venezuela	21,738
Senegal	8,102	Peru	23,331
Sweden	8,735	Kenya	26,017

SOURCE: Statistics Canada; *The World Bank Atlas 1996.*

189

28

The More Moderate Option
of Partial Withdrawal

It's important to remember exactly what we're talking about here. It's what the rest of us would do if the Yes side did win a next referendum in Quebec, by the modest or even bare majority that seems closest to a realistic possibility at the moment.

And again, even though this would almost certainly not be enough to make threats of unilateral secession an effective bargaining chip for any PQ government of Quebec, it would at least render all continuing talk about "renewed federalism" or "unique character" or "giving more powers to all the provinces" quite pointless. Overnight, everything would suddenly change.

Learning to love sovereignty-association

In principle, the rest of us *could* just do nothing. We could just sit back and dare the PQ government to secede unilaterally, with some confidence that it would only fail if it tried.

In practice, however, we too would be plunged into the vast confusion of the black hole. And, as I've already noted, we and all our savings and investments and other practical plans for the future would have a viscerally immediate interest in getting out of the thing, as quickly as we could.

In this setting, I think it's probably true enough that we'd have no practical choice but to find some way of talking with the PQ government of Quebec about the "sovereignty-partnership" or "sovereignty-association" concept, that has been the recurrent underlying objective of the Quebec sovereigntist movement, ever since René Lévesque founded the Parti Québécois in 1968. And if we do want to make sure that we don't wind up as the dog that gets wagged by its tail in this circumstance, we ought to be figuring out in advance just what kind of sovereignty-association arrangement would make the most sense from our own point of view (or, one might more nobly say, from the standpoint of the people of Canada at large, from coast to coast to coast).

In fact, during the 1997 federal election campaign, the editor-in-chief of Canada's national newspaper (with whose views I don't always agree myself) wrote a provocative opinion piece that quite explicitly drew attention to the logic of this position. "Sovereignty-association," he argued, is the "Plan D" of the current great debate, and "the black sheep" that has received "very little attention in the English-speaking part" of Canada so far. Yet "could we really refuse to talk if Quebeckers voted unambiguously for the ambiguity of sovereignty-association?"* (And, at the bottom of everything, this really is the question that has been voted on in both the 1980 and 1995 Quebec referendums, and that would almost certainly be voted on in any next referendum, organized in any near future by the Parti Québécois.)

Why the Quebec concept won't work

One reason sovereignty-association has received so little attention outside Quebec is that the particular version of the arrangement envisioned by the Quebec sovereigntist movement is so unambiguously unattractive for the rest of the country. Ted himself once told me that "the PQ's idea of sovereignty-association makes absolutely no sense for any part of Canada except Quebec." And I think this is no less than the simple truth.

More exactly, I think it's fair to say that all the concepts of some new partnership or association with the rest of the country which the Quebec sovereigntist movement has broached publicly over the past few decades have two features that go beyond the pale of serious discussion in any other part of Canada. The first is a notion of "equal partnership" that can only be judged anything but equal, from the standpoint of anyone who does not

---

*William Thorsell, "The referendum question Ottawa is working hard to disqualify," *The Globe and Mail*, May 17, 1997, D6. For those who find the various lettered "plans" that have been popularly discussed in the last few years intriguing, "Plan A" is renewed federalism, "unique character," and all that; "Plan B" is "tough-love terms" for "negotiating Quebec's independence"; and "Plan C" is, or perhaps used to be, "Preston Manning's term for the Reform Party's 'new federalism'" (giving all provinces "more powers").

live in Quebec. And the second is what amounts to yet another complicated level of government, in a rather thinly populated part of the world that already has at least as many complicated levels of government as it can manage or needs.

As best as I can tell, in any case, the version of sovereignty-association proposed by the Quebec sovereigntist movement assumes that two new democratic national states would somehow be created – one called "Quebec" (which includes all of the present Canadian province of Quebec), and one called "Canada" (which includes all of the rest of present-day Canada).

These two new national states would then associate, or forge a new partnership, under a "supranational" arrangement (lately the supposedly analogous experience of the new European Union is often invoked), within which each of the two new states would have equal representation. In the management of this new supranational structure, in other words, the somewhat less than 25% of the present Canadian population that lives in Quebec would have the same power as the somewhat more than 75% of the population that lives in the rest of the country.

Even non-sovereigntist Quebec francophones (Lysiane Gagnon, who sometimes writes a column from Montreal for Canada's national newspaper, immediately comes to mind) concede that the rest of us would have to be very great chumps indeed to agree to any arrangement of this sort. And I wouldn't even try to explain why the Quebec sovereigntist leadership continues to behave as if it were even a remotely credible or realistic proposal.

At the same time, I suppose I can very dimly imagine that, if *I* were a Quebec sovereigntist, I might just be able to delude myself into thinking that it is good politics to propose such an arrangement, as the opening gambit in some much more serious round of negotiations, with bargaining partners who have never yet been inclined to be serious themselves, about anything I have tried to say for more than an entire generation.

An alternative concept

My own key assumption here is that a PQ government of Quebec, which had just won a next referendum by something in the order of 52%, actually would be open enough to an alternative concept of sovereignty-association, proposed by the rest of the country in the interest of the Canada born in the fur trade, from coast to coast to coast. (I'll talk about the options for the rest of us if this assumption were to prove false shortly: for the moment I just want to proceed as if it were essentially correct.)

As it happens, I think there is an alternative concept of this sort. And I'm drawing in particular on at least some elements in a body of ideas proposed most notably by University of British Columbia professor of political science, Philip Resnick, some time ago now, in the wake of the failure of the Meech Lake Accord.*

The details of implementing this alternative concept of sovereignty-association (or new partnership between Quebec and the rest of Canada) could no doubt become complicated enough. And they would be subject to more than enough tortuous negotiation to satisfy the most ardent professional constitutional sportsperson. But the general concept itself seems to me quite simple. Put in abstract terms, the present Canadian province of Quebec would not even pretend to "secede" but would merely "withdraw partially" from the present Canadian federal system. *And for every degree, as it were, that it withdrew from the system, it would lose a commensurate degree of influence over the system's management and operation.* It would never withdraw completely or altogether, however, and the present structure and historic geographic unity of Canada would remain intact.

I am assuming that at least a Parti Québécois government of Quebec would want to pursue this process of partial withdrawal some considerable distance – to the point where, for most ordinary purposes of day-to-day government, Quebec residents do constitute a democratic people of Quebec, separate from the people of Canada (as the people of no other current Canadian province are or, I am assuming again, would want to be). Yet for

---

*Philip Resnick, *Toward a Canada-Quebec Union* (Montreal and Kingston: McGill-Queen's University Press, 1991). In fact, I think what I'm doing is adapting certain parts of this book to the principle of sovereignty-association, but of course I could be wrong. I've found parts of another book helpful as well: Anthony Westell, *Reinventing Canada* (Toronto: Dundurn Press, 1994).

a limited number of certain other purposes, Quebec residents would remain part of the people of Canada, and continue to enjoy some limited representation in the Canadian federal parliament. One key question is whether the resulting new sovereign national state of Quebec could and would apply for its own seat in the United Nations. And my view of the sovereignty-association concept involved is that, in principle, it could.[*]

Negotiating the partial withdrawal

Of course a new sovereign Quebec that did want its own seat in the United Nations would have to forego a very great deal of its present influence over the Canadian federal system. And, like every other part of the ultimate concrete arrangements, this would be subject to negotiations with the rest of the country.

As Ted once explained to me at length, the only practicable forum for negotiations of this sort would involve essentially the same group that negotiated the failed Charlottetown Accord of 1992 – the First Ministers of the Canadian federal and present ten provincial governments (perhaps supplemented, as at Charlottetown, by some representation of aboriginal groups and the northern territories, at the First Ministers' discretion).

As I've implied earlier, in principle (or, if you like, in theory), the First Ministers' forum is not an ideal negotiating body. While the provincial government of Quebec might plausibly be said to represent Quebec's interests, the federal and other nine provincial governments constitute a flawed representative for the rest of the country. (To take just the most blatant case, if a next referendum were held during the term of the federal government elected in 1997, the first minister of Canada would represent both "Canada" at large *and* a federal constituency inside "Quebec.")

At the same time, the negotiations are *not* about the secession of Quebec (*or* the creation of some new supranational institution

---

[*]There are somewhat strained but quite real precedents for constituent parts of federal member-states of the United Nations to have their own separate UN seats. When the UN was established in 1945, two constituent "union republics" of the Union of Soviet Socialist Republics – Byelorussia (the present Belarus) and the Ukraine – had their own UN seats, along with the USSR itself.

by two new national states), but merely about Quebec's partial withdrawal from the present federal system: so the *present* federal government must be represented, even in principle.

Moreover, the practical difficulties of promptly constituting some more credible representative for the rest of the country, in the midst of the black hole, are so enormous as to make the First Ministers' forum an acceptable enough compromise. And in both theory and practice, the negotiations would be subject to the present Canadian constitutional amending formula.

Again, Quebec is just withdrawing *partially* from a federal system that otherwise remains as it is now. The federal government could make no deal with Quebec without the support of at least six (and in some cases all) provinces outside Quebec.

The very last referendum

The PQ government of Quebec would have its own problems with this negotiating forum. It would prefer to deal with some single partner, not with the present federal and nine other provincial governments. In the first instance, Ottawa and the nine other provinces may find it convenient to designate some single negotiating team. Ultimately, however, just as there is no practicable alternative to the First Ministers' forum for the rest of the country, there would be no alternative for Quebec.

The ultimate democratic protection for everyone's interests is that whatever exact new sovereignty-association deal the First Ministers' forum finally came up with would have to be ratified in a very last popular referendum, involving all present citizens of Canada, from coast to coast to coast.

This would be required by the precedent of the failed Charlottetown Accord, by provincial legislation already on the books in BC and Alberta, and by sheer common sense. Those directly involved in First Ministers' negotiations would also be under constant pressure to ensure – through opinion polling and ordinary democratic debate – that whatever they finally did come up with had virtually certain prospects of winning such an ultimate referendum, in Canada at large.

Failure at this stage would only plunge all of us still deeper into the black hole. And it would be the height of irresponsibility for negotiators representing the *people* of Canada and Quebec, not themselves or their narrow bureaucratic interests, to risk such an altogether ominous fate. (Politicians, as my brother would point out, are irresponsible in this way almost by nature: but one could only hope that the gravity of the situation would call forth unnatural behaviour on everyone's part.)

How a negotiated new deal might look

Of course it is impossible to predict in advance just what the detailed results of such sovereignty-association negotiations might be. All one can say is that Canada is blessed with many people who have decided talents for working out the details of such things – the heirs, as it were, of those Arthur Lower had in mind, when he wrote that: "No group of men could frame a better set of exchange regulations." Yet I suppose that what Ted would call "some concrete image" of a resulting new arrangement can be suggested, as a guide to the concept.

We might assume here, for instance, that Quebec would withdraw from the present Canadian federal system with respect to virtually all ordinary domestic functions of government. For most purposes, Quebec residents would constitute a new democratic people of Quebec. Following the Quebec sovereigntist model, they would pay taxes only to the government of Quebec. And there would be a commensurate drastic reduction in Quebec's influence over the Canadian federal system, to the point where it would no longer send any elected representatives to the so-called "lower house" of the federal or "Canadian national" parliament (known now, and presumably – though not necessarily – in the future as well, as the House of Commons).*

At the same time, Quebec residents would continue to be part of the people of Canada with respect to a few very high functions

---

*During the dying days of the Meech Lake Accord, a highly educated cab driver of West Indian descent, in Calgary, told me that, so long as so much else about the constitution was being changed, the name "House of Commons" was a British colonial vestige that ought to be replaced. I would be pleased to see the name replaced myself, though by exactly what I don't know.

of government, such as currency and coinage, central banking, international (and certainly interprovincial) trade, and – with perhaps some degree of qualification – foreign policy and defence. Some particular or special responsibility for these functions would be assigned to a reformed upper house of the federal parliament (known now as the Senate), and Quebec would send a number of representatives to this reformed upper house, *proportionate to its share of the Canada-wide population.*

These Quebec senators would only have power to deal with those few functions of government with respect to which Quebec residents remained part of the people of Canada. They would be selected by the new sovereign government of Quebec, via a method of its own choosing. This could be popular election but would, I'd guess, more likely involve some form of appointment by what is even now known as the Assemblée nationale of Quebec. The government of Quebec would remit an annual payment to the government of Canada, to cover all costs associated with the Quebec senators – and with the administration of those few functions of government with respect to which Quebec residents remained part of the people of Canada

Personally, I would argue against any other formal or constitutional relationship between the new sovereign government of Quebec and the government of Canada. It is only reasonable to anticipate, however, that various informal habits of interaction between the prime minister of the new Quebec and the prime minister of Canada would gradually put down roots.

With respect to this last office itself, Walt has told me that in the history of the old British dominion of Canada there actually is a case of a senator from Quebec (John Abbott) serving briefly as prime minister of Canada (1891–92). And, again, my assumption is that, except for the changes I've just discussed (and a few other optional or conceivable prospects discussed immediately below), Canada would carry on constitutionally as it has since 1867 (and 1982). Yet the very limited powers of Quebec senators under the new arrangements would make it extremely awkward for one of their number to serve as a prime minister of Canada. The reasonable anticipation here is that, as at present, Canadian prime ministers would typically be drawn from the lower house of the federal parliament, in which Quebec would no longer have any representatives at all.

Exhibit 39
"Can't Get No Satisfaction," March 1996

"In general, would you say that you are satisfied or dissatisfied with the direction in which this country is going?"

Region	% No Opinion	% Satisfied	% Dissatisfied
Quebec	**5**	**18**	**78**
Atlantic Canada	10	26	64
Prairies	9	33	58
Ontario	8	36	56
British Columbia	12	34	54
CANADA	**8**	**30**	**62**

SOURCE: Gallup Poll Canada.

29

Partition and the Worst-Case Scenario

This particular concrete image of a new sovereignty-association deal between Quebec and the rest of Canada can also be viewed as a benchmark, from which movement in opposite directions is possible. Negotiations of the sort I've just suggested could lead to a new sovereign Quebec that was more closely tied to the rest of the country than the benchmark implies. Or, through some unfortunate process of breakdown, they could lead to some form of actual *negotiated secession* of Quebec, ultimately agreed to by all parties – and ratified in a Canada-wide referendum.*

As I've said before (or should have, if I haven't), I'm no constitutional expert, and I wouldn't pretend to have thought through all the possible permutations and combinations in this connection. I don't really see how anyone could do such a thing in advance: you can reduce the risks of the black hole by figuring out what you would do yourself, but "you" are never the only negotiating partner, and the black hole will always be there. I do have some quick reflections to offer on two particular cases, however (one in each of the two directions, as it were), by way of rounding out my thoughts on the subject at large.

Being realistic about partition

I've talked with some people who were surprised that, in the immediate wake of the 1995 referendum, certain groups among the anglophone and aboriginal minorities in Quebec suddenly raised the prospect of "partitioning" the province, in the event that Quebec actually did *secede* from Canada.

This drew in part on Pierre Trudeau's ancient argument that "if Canada is divisible, so is Quebec." And even Jean Chrétien's constitutional point person, Stéphane Dion (somewhat ironically,

---

*This also sharply raises what seems to be the most popular subject in discussions about Quebec secession: the division of Canada's present national debt (which would be something of an issue in "partial withdrawal" as well).

the son of the same Lion Dion who once talked about holding a knife to the rest of the country's throat) has voiced a certain theoretical sympathy for the concept of partition, on behalf of the present federal government in Ottawa.

The concept envisions that if the present geographic territory of Quebec were to secede from Canada, then certain geographic subdivisions of this territory (in the west and north, where anglophones and aboriginals are numerically prominent in the population) would secede from Quebec and remain in Canada.

In fact, the Quebec that joined the present federal system in 1867 did not have as vast a geography as it has today. And at least in the northern part of the province the partition argument can find some theoretical support in Canadian history.

As a practical matter, however, all theoretical talk of this sort strikes me as an all-too-deadly business. Elsewhere in the history of the world, some decidedly unhappy territorial partitions have accompanied the creation of new national states. The division of the old British Raj in South Asia into India and Pakistan, after the Second World War, prompted a tragic wave of political violence. The partition of Ireland after the First World War spawned a tradition of political violence that still thrives today.

In the end, I don't see how the Canadian federal government could retain part of Quebec's present territory, in the event of an actual secession, without resorting to armed force. If *secession* ever did become the real issue, only people insane enough to risk death in a violent Canadian civil war would still be talking about the partition of Quebec. And practically, again, I doubt that any significant number of other people would listen to this talk.

Another more moderate approach

Having said all this, I also think I can see how talk about partition does appeal to a certain sense of justice. And it seems to me that there may be some room to accommodate this sense of justice – and to strengthen the association between a sovereign Quebec and the rest of Canada – in more moderate negotiations on Quebec's partial withdrawal from the present federal system.

To start with, residents within certain comparatively modest fragments of a new sovereign Quebec's territory (in northern Quebec or the west end of Montreal, for instance) might continue to pay some taxes to the federal government, receive some federal services in return, and perhaps even continue to enjoy some representation in the lower house of the federal parliament.*

To give this option some serious countervailing attraction for a new sovereign Quebec, the predominantly French-speaking residents within certain comparatively modest fragments of the territory in the rest of Canada – in northern New Brunswick or eastern and northeastern Ontario, and perhaps some parts of Manitoba, for instance – might also have some of their federal taxes directed to the government of Quebec, and receive some services from the government of Quebec in return. (And, following a parallel logic, they might acquire some representation in the Assemblée nationale of Quebec as well.)

Frankly, I have absolutely no idea just how practicable or politically possible arrangements of this sort might prove to be – particularly in the midst of the black hole that a Yes victory in a next Quebec referendum would pitch everyone into, and the no doubt many harsh and bitter feelings that would do so much to make the black hole an unpleasant place. Yet I do think that some version of such a scheme could do a lot both to strengthen any association between a new sovereign Quebec and the rest of Canada, and to help keep alive the historic geographic unity of the Canada that was born in the fur trade, from coast to coast to coast. And I would warmly endorse any such scheme that did prove practicable and politically possible myself.

What if secession proved inevitable after all?

For reasons somewhat similar to those I've discussed in the case of unilateral secession, I still can't quite bring myself to believe that even a negotiated version of an actual full-bodied secession of Quebec from Canada is all that likely. I do think Veronica and

---

*In this case it would also continue to be *theoretically* possible, though still extremely unlikely in practice, for someone such as Paul Martin, for example, to serve as a prime minister of Canada, representing a constituency in Quebec.

her friends (and Jean Chrétien or Jean Charest) are right, when they argue that this is just not what anything remotely approaching a majority of Quebecers today really wants.

Yet I also suspect that it would be a great mistake to underestimate the infinite danger of the black hole. As I've already noted, even with the latest efforts of the provincial premiers and Stéphane Dion, I do think there's a reasonable enough prospect of a next referendum in Quebec, and a fair enough chance that the Yes side could win it by something in the order of 52%. That alone would pitch all of us into the black hole. And once we're in the black hole, I'd reluctantly agree that the prospects of some form of *negotiated secession* are far from negligible.

It *seems* clear that *some* factions of the Quebec sovereigntist leadership would be happy just to have Quebec secede altogether from Canada, regardless of what may or may not happen to the rest of the country, or of any relationship a completely independent Quebec may or may not have with whatever were to become of Canada in the future. (And Jacques Parizeau, with his lobsters in the pot, his unused TV tape of a victory address to the universe, and his advisors in France has often enough appeared perilously close to a case in point.)

Moreover, it *is* some version of the present Quebec sovereigntist leadership – not the people of Quebec at large, or non-sovereigntist newspaper columnists who write for Canada's national newspaper, or even some representative sample of the Assemblée nationale – that would be involved in any negotiations with the federal and nine other provincial governments, following a Yes side victory in a next referendum.

Alas, I myself am not altogether confident that my earlier assumption – about how a PQ government that had just won a Yes vote would be open to more moderate negotiations on partial withdrawal from the Canadian federal system – is correct. And it does seem true that negotiations of this sort would never quite give the Quebec sovereigntist leadership exactly what it has traditionally said *it* wants out of a sovereignty-association deal.

(And, besides, even if you ignore the crucial democratic issue of linguistic majorities, Quebec *is* different. To take just one of many possible cases in point, more than twice as many cohabiting couples in Quebec, comparatively speaking, are nowadays living "common law" or, as it used to be said, "without benefit of clergy," as in the rest of Canada at large.)

Lament for two nations

It often seems to me as well that opinion of virtually all political persuasions in francophone Quebec is still not fully aware of just how seminally exasperated opinion on the so-called great Canadian debate has become, in virtually all parts of the rest of the country. I also think that much of the media in English-speaking Canada is still all-too-nobly filtering out and trying to repress rather more of this exasperation than is probably healthy – and I say this as someone who, reluctantly but resolutely, voted for the Liberal Party of Canada in the 1997 federal election.

I would certainly guess that there are vast numbers of people in the rest of Canada who would be prepared to ratify some negotiated full-bodied secession of Quebec in an ultimate referendum, if the only alternative were the 25%-is-equal-to-75% association deal traditionally advocated by the sovereigntist movement in Quebec. And, as the Quebec reaction to the failure of Meech Lake suggests, the rejection of one perceived insult in the rest of the country could easily be taken as an insult in francophone Quebec, a decisive majority of which would then also be prepared to ratify a negotiated secession.

And so, even though nothing close to a majority in either place really wanted it, the actual secession of Quebec *is* what we could all get in the end. Far stranger things have happened in the history of the world, and I know quite sensible people who are more pessimistic about human nature than I am, who do believe that this is the most likely outcome even of a 52% Yes vote in a next Quebec referendum. As I've said, I still can't believe it is all that likely myself. But I do agree it could happen.

If it did happen, I don't think the rest of us would have any alternative but to try to carry on with what was left of Canada's historic geographic unity as best we could – having first ensured in our negotiations with the seceding Quebec that we had the kind of deal which would create the best possible prospects for our own survival. (And meanwhile, of course again, more than a few among us would likely enough be dusting off our résumés for the Congress in Washington, just in case this also proved necessary, in the absolute end.)

Exhibit 40
Percentage of Couples in Common-Law Unions Canada and Its Provinces, 1981, 1995
(What can this possibly mean?)

	1981 (%)	1995 (%)
Quebec	**8.2**	**25.0**
British Columbia	7.9	13.8
Alberta	7.7	12.2
Atlantic provinces	3.9	11.2
Ontario	5.0	9.9
Manitoba and Saskatchewan	4.7	7.1
Rest of Canada	**5.6**	**10.7**
CANADA	6.3	14.3

SOURCE: Statistics Canada.

30

Making Federalism
in Nine Provinces Work

As I think almost everyone outside Quebec would probably agree, the most distressing implication of an actual secession of Quebec from Canada – unilateral or negotiated – is how it would fracture the historic geographic unity of northern North America.

It is true enough that Alaska and Hawaii are geographically separated from the lower forty-eight states of the USA, much as Atlantic Canada would be separated from Canada west of the Ottawa River by an altogether independent Quebec. Yet in a country like Canada today, whose people can only be united by their geographic descent – and whose uniqueness has so much to do with the rugged ecological romance of its vast wilderness geography, from coast to coast to coast – the loss of a strategically located 15 to 16% of the historic national territory could well prove to be a psychic wound of devastating proportions.[*]

At the same time, the long-term survival of the present provinces and territories of Canada outside Quebec also raises a rather different set of more practical political problems. And while these problems would surface in their most intense form in the case of a "rest of Canada" that tried to survive on its own, after some full-bodied secession of Quebec, they would arise in a somewhat less-intense form as well, even in the case of a successful sovereignty-association deal, based on the principle of Quebec's partial withdrawal from the present federal system.

Ted himself has once again offered the most succinct summary of the issue here that I've heard myself: "For some people,"

---

[*]And the strictly *English-speaking cultural* side of the rest of the country's identity does not help here: if that is what is most important, then the sensible thing to do *is* to join the USA. Similarly, if the *French-speaking cultural* side of a sovereign Quebec's identity really is secondary to geographic descent within Quebec's present borders, then partition movements in the wake of secession could also prove devastating for an independent Quebec.

he told me over lunch a while ago, "the presence of no or almost no representatives from Quebec in the lower house of the federal parliament probably would improve the way things are now in one respect, but it would only make them worse in another."

Would other provinces want to withdraw partially too?

The most neutral way of approaching this particular set of problems, I think, is to focus on the currently rather overwhelming population (in comparative terms) of Canada's most-populous province of Ontario. There is a somewhat trickier path to the same door, however, that ought to be dealt with first.

The point of departure along this trickier path is the abstract principle of the equality of the provinces in the Canadian federation. (And in fact this principle, one might argue, has become as prominent as it has over the past several decades of Canadian constitutional wrangling, because it does serve to protect everyone else from Ontario's rather overwhelming population – or the even more overwhelming population of the two old central Canadian conspirators of Ontario and Quebec together.)

If Quebec is going to be "allowed" to withdraw partially from the Canadian federal system, as part of some new sovereignty-association deal, strong advocates of the provincial equality principle are immediately inclined to argue that every other province should have this option as well. And of course if every province were to pick up the option, there would be no more Canadian federal system from which to withdraw. In fact, it seems quite clear to me that if even only one other province apart from Quebec were to pick up the option, the entire sovereignty-association project would no longer work. (If nothing else, the population of Canada at large *is* just too comparatively small.)

In terms of the principle of provincial equality, in any case, the whole point of the sovereignty-association concept is that, while the principle does apply to the other nine provinces, it cannot and does not apply to Quebec. And the ultimate logic here is that *in each of the other nine provinces the majority of the population only knows how to speak English, while in Quebec the majority of the population only knows how to speak French.* The majorities in the nine other provinces can democratically communicate with each other in the same language, but the majority in Quebec cannot democratically communicate with the other majorities in this way (and so it cannot be the same or "equal" to them in the federation).

Moreover, in the scenario of partial withdrawal from the federal system that I've been sketching here, the rest of us are only going to accept Quebec's rejection of the principle of provincial equality for itself – and are only going to start negotiating a sovereignty-association deal based on the concept of partial withdrawal – because at least a bare but clear majority of the Quebec electorate actually has voted Yes in a sovereignty referendum. So, even if one were to argue that there are distinctions other than linguistic difference which might prompt claims to the "right" of partial withdrawal in other provinces, for a province to "win" or "earn" this right in the eyes of the rest of the country, at least a bare but clear majority of its electorate would also have to vote Yes in a sovereignty referendum.

It seems to me that the problem of Quebec in Canada today is finally about the relationship between historical experience and the rise of a new democracy, rather than the relationship between the rise of a new democracy and abstract rights. But if you do try to put the concept of sovereignty-association for Quebec in the context of abstract rights about provincial equality, some such requirement for accompanying sovereignty referendums strikes me as the ultimate abstract logic. And is there really any provincial government in Canada, other than a Parti Québécois government of Quebec, that would be remotely prepared to go to the trouble of holding such referendums? And even if there were, would anyone *really* want to bet any of their hard-earned Canadian dollars on the prospect that the Yes side would win?

The real issue: too many people in Ontario

All this, alas, is merely a clever argument (or at least so it seems to me) that finally has nothing to do with the real practical political problems which even the partial withdrawal of Quebec would lay at the door of the remaining full and equal provincial partners in the Canadian federal system.

As matters stand now, Quebec has somewhat less than 25% of the total Canadian population, and Ontario has rather more than one-third. But in day-to-day political practice (as opposed to the most aggressive ideologies of regional alienation), French-English cultural conflict between Ontario and Quebec, and the traditional commercial rivalry between Toronto and Montreal, has tended to moderate at least Ontario's worst impulses towards dominance in the Canadian confederation at large.

Yet once Quebec were to withdraw from the present federal system, to the extent that it inevitably would in any serious new sovereignty-association deal, there would be a vast new area of Canadian federal government and politics which would involve only the nine provinces and soon-to-be-three territories outside Quebec. As I've already alluded to, for instance, in the "concrete image" of a new deal I sketched earlier, the lower house of the federal parliament would have no or almost no members from Quebec. And the relevant alarming demographic statistic in this context is that Ontario alone has just under 50% of the total population of "Canada without Quebec" – and would thus have close to half the seats in the new Canadian House of Commons (or whatever else it may be called).

Thus people like Gordon Wilson in British Columbia have already warned that, if a majority of Quebecers do vote Yes in a next referendum, the "central Canadian establishment" in Ottawa ought not to expect that BC will just fall into line with some Ontario-dominated rest-of-Canada strategy. They are pointing to what strike me as highly understandable concerns about the almost overwhelming demographic might of Ontario, in any Canadian federal system in which Quebec no longer played its present role. I suspect that other strong provincial equality advocates, who argue every province ought to have the same "right" to sovereignty-association as Quebec, are ultimately only voicing similar concerns. And I have no doubt at all that this is an utterly crucial issue, which would have to be resolved, in one way or another, to make any kind of new sovereignty-association deal with Quebec work in the rest of the country.

Is BC really British California?

One way of at least addressing (if not quite resolving) the current demographic dominance of Ontario in Canada outside Quebec is to point to long-term population growth prospects. The populations of both BC and Alberta have actually been growing at a considerably faster *rate* than Ontario's population in the past generation. And it is not unreasonable to argue that Ontario's current demographic dominance is not going to last forever.*

Following the well-established Canadian habit of looking south of the undefended border for inspiration in such matters, for example, it is at least intriguing that the relationship between the populations of BC and Ontario in 1991 was almost identical to that between California and New York State in 1920. In round numbers BC had about 3.4 million people in 1991, and Ontario had about 10.5 million. In 1920 California had about 3.4 million people and New York State had about 10.4 million. Some half a century later, in 1970, the population of California was actually greater than that of New York State. And it may well be that the population of BC will actually be greater than the population of Ontario by the middle of the twenty-first century.

At the same time, calculations of this sort are inherently uncertain, and depend on factors that no one can seriously predict. A variety of arguments can be advanced to the effect that the historic relationship between California and New York State in the US is just not the same as that between BC and Ontario in the Canadian future. Ontario has been Canada's most-populous province ever since the present confederation began in 1867, and its share of the Canada-wide population is actually somewhat greater today than it was in the 1950s.

Western Canadian population growth has also proved quite volatile in the past. In the 1920s Saskatchewan was Canada's third most-populous province, and Winnipeg, Manitoba, was the country's third most-populous city. Both Manitoba and Saskatchewan have subsequently fallen on harder times, while Ontario has

---

*Between 1961 and 1991, BC's population more than doubled, and Alberta's almost doubled, while Ontario's only increased by some 68%.

just kept on growing. Even today both BC and Alberta still have traditionally Canadian resource-dominated economies, subject to a wide range of unpredictable fluctuations. If I were a resident of either place – and, as I've already noted, it strikes me that I just may finish my life as a resident of BC – I would at least think twice before I listened too hard to any talk about the naturally fading demographic dominance of Ontario, in any Canadian federal system in which Quebec was only a very modest and part-time partner, in a small room at the top of the stairs.

The fantasy of deconstructing Ontario

In the very end, and despite the obsolescence of the Laurentian thesis, free trade, the rise of the Pacific Rim, and the death of the old national business class, I think a not insignificant case can still be made for Harold Innis's old 1930s view that the "strength of Ontario may emphasize the weakness of the federation." And I suspect that a successful new sovereignty-association deal with Quebec would require at least a few extraordinary efforts by both the federal and provincial branches of Ontario's current political leadership, at putting Canada first in the rest of the country.

The obvious-enough crux of the problem is that any nine-province federal system, where one province has about half the population of the system at large, is going to present some recurrent managerial and practical political problems of a quite tall order. As Ted himself also argued the last time I was in Ottawa, if this sort of system hopes to achieve any long-term stability, it will ultimately have to either reconfigure itself, or create some mechanism to offset the excessive demographic weight of its one (comparatively) gargantuan province.

It seems to me equally obvious that some form of reconfiguration would be the most theoretically attractive but also most practically challenging and difficult option. And the obvious move here would be to either decrease or increase the number of provinces in the system. Equally obviously again, increasing the number, by dividing Ontario itself into, say, four new provinces, would attack the fundamental problem most directly.

Given the rampant restructuring in other directions that the

Harris government has already begun to unleash on Canada's most-populous province, "deconstructing" the present Ontario into a few smaller provincial units may not be quite as radical and inconceivable a prospect as it may have seemed even just a few years ago. But I agree with Ted that, in practice, the black hole opened up by a Yes vote in Quebec would still have to get very dark indeed for anything of this sort to happen in the real world.

A more realistic approach to Senate reform

The more likely prospect, no doubt, involves creating some new mechanism in the wider institutions of the Canadian federal system, that would offset Ontario's overbearing demographic weight in the lower house of the federal parliament. And the most obvious approach in this direction would involve some additional layer of restructuring in the reformed federal Senate, that would also be serving as a vehicle for the continued representation of Quebec, for those few functions of government with respect to which Quebec residents remained part of the people of Canada.

Anyone foolish enough to have paid a great deal of attention to the Charlottetown Accord may be reminded of what happened to Alberta's proposal for so-called "triple E" Senate reform in that context. As best as I can tell from the newspapers, since then at least some influential individuals in both Alberta and British Columbia have come to realize that they actually live in "large" not "small" provinces. And they have acquired some fresh doubts about the pure principle of equal provincial representation in a reformed Senate (in the sovereignty-association case, of course, for the nine provinces but not for Quebec).

More exactly, along with Ontario, both Alberta and BC would presumably continue to contribute some form of equalization payments to Atlantic Canada and Manitoba and Saskatchewan (though of course, again, no longer to Quebec). And a pure provincially equal Senate with real general power in a new nine-province federal system – as well as some particular powers regarding those few functions of government with respect to which Quebec residents remained part of the people of Canada – could ultimately just become a perpetual lobby for increasing equalization payments to unconscionably exorbitant levels.

I would nonetheless assume that, if Ontario is not quite prepared to deconstruct itself into a few smaller provinces, both Alberta and BC (along with the rest of both western and Atlantic Canada) would continue, understandably enough, to demand some form of counterweight to Ontario's overbearing demographic weight in the lower house of the federal parliament. I would guess that the most logical place for this counterweight would continue to be in some version of the same reformed Senate, that would also serve as the continuing institutional link with the new sovereign national state of Quebec. And Ontario would ultimately have no choice but to meet the demand.

Put another way, the formula for provincial representation in this reformed Senate starts with the principle that Quebec is not a province like the others. So it gets a number of seats proportionate to its population. At the same time, all the other provinces, *collectively*, get a number of seats proportionate to their collective population. The trick from here is to allocate these seats among the non-Quebec provinces, so as to recognize *both* that each province *is* in principle equal to the others, *and* that the "large" (or equalization-paying) provinces must have greater representation than the "small" (or equalization-receiving) provinces, to ensure that there is some appropriate degree of equity and justice in the continuing equalization system, among all nine full and equal provinces outside Quebec.

To take just a quick and arbitrary *example*, a 48-member reformed Senate might have 12, as it were, part-time members from Quebec, 6 full-time members from each of BC, Alberta, and Ontario, and 3 full-time members from each of the other six provinces. And, to tie everything up in one neat bow at the end, a crucial function of such a reformed Senate of Canada (or Canada and Quebec) would be to serve as a focal point for the development of exactly the new kind of Canadian national economic policy (or, from Quebec's standpoint, Canadian economic-space policy) that Ted feels is going to be so important for the future – a new Canadian national economic policy, that is, which works as well for the rest of the country, as it works for the old Laurentian-empire provinces of Ontario and Quebec.

HOW TO SURVIVE
IF NOTHING HAPPENS
AT ALL

Exhibit 41
How "Can't Get No Satisfaction" Can Change
All Canada, Various Dates, 1973–1996

"In general, would you say that you are satisfied or dissatisfied with the direction in which this country is going?"

Date	% No Opinion	% Satisfied	% Dissatisfied
Jul 1982	7	12	81
Feb 1991	5	15	80
Jul 1992	4	20	76
Jun 1990	7	22	71
Nov 1981	13	23	64
Mar 1978	14	22	64
Jul 1983	9	28	63
Mar 1996	8	30	62
Nov 1980	11	30	59
Sep 1994	6	36	58
Mar 1995	9	36	55
Jan 1973	20	42	38

SOURCE: Gallup Poll Canada.

31

What Did the 1995 Referendum Mean?

As I've already noted, what most impressed my sister about the 1995 Quebec referendum was just how many people – and especially just how many so-called Quebec francophones – did vote No, even then.

It is also a simple mathematical truth that if all unilingual Quebec francophones were to vote Yes in a sovereignty referendum, the Yes side would win handily enough. Yet after some three decades of more-or-less relentless effort – and two referendum questions that have quite deliberately included explicit references to some continuing association or partnership between a sovereign Quebec and the rest of Canada – there are still substantial numbers of even unilingual francophone Quebecers who reject the Quebec sovereigntist movement. And I agree with Veronica that this does raise some questions about the movement's long-term future.

I also agree with Veronica that, as I'm writing, both the recent history of opinion polls about support for sovereignty in Quebec, and the results of the 1997 federal election leave rather more than a little room for wondering about just how well the Yes side might actually do in a next referendum. And of course, once again, there is some room for wondering about whether a next referendum will even take place.

The upshot of all this is that, while I am now somewhat less confused than I was when I began setting my reflections about the future of Canada and Quebec down on paper, I also remain (like a great many other people, no doubt) somewhat confused. Unlike Veronica, I am almost on the verge of believing that some form of "sovereign Quebec," for want of better words, is almost inevitable. But it will (or would) take at least some kind of actual Yes-side majority in a next referendum to convince me altogether, and remove every last one of my remaining doubts.

Was 1995 the peak or just a mid-point in the sovereigntist trajectory?

In fact Veronica is not the only person I know who argues that the 49.4% Yes vote in the 1995 Quebec referendum represented a historic peak in support for sovereignty (or, more exactly, sovereignty-association or sovereignty-partnership), the likes of which we will never see again. My wife, it turns out, believes that there will be a next referendum, but that the Yes side will lose once more and the issue of Canada and Quebec's future will continue to fester unresolved. (She would, she says, prefer to see a Yes-side victory, followed by "some deal like you're talking about," but she does not think that is what will happen.)

Veronica (you will probably not be surprised to hear) believes that if only the rest of the country would show some willingness to revisit the sort of "moderate accommodation" first broached in the failed Meech Lake Accord, the Quebec Liberal Party could handily enough defeat the Parti Québécois in the next Quebec provincial election. Then there would be no need for a next referendum, and the sovereigntist movement would start a slow but sure decline into ultimate obscurity. ("All I'm saying," Veronica assures me, "is some formal recognition of what Quebec has actually become." And she told me over the phone a few days ago that she is "cautiously optimistic" about the process launched by the provincial premiers in the late summer of 1997.)

On the other side of the fence, I also know people who believe that there almost certainly will be a next referendum in Quebec ("by the early twenty-first century, in any case"), and that the Yes side probably will win by some comparatively slender majority, and then "God knows what will happen." Strangely enough, it was Ted himself who finally uttered these exact words, the last time I was in Ottawa. My wife and I were having dinner, at a bar on Elgin Street, with Ted and Veronica, and Madeleine and Walt, the night before we came back home. To some extent, I think, Ted was just giving Veronica the hard time she so often richly deserves, as an intimate amusement. But he still said a number of things that impressed me.

What we should remember about the opinion polls on sovereignty in Quebec, Ted argued, was that they always go up and down, and that "what most francophone Quebecers think of as renewed or reformed federalism is largely what the rest of us think of as sovereignty-association in any case." The 1995 referendum itself showed that, when it gets its act together, the sovereigntist movement can command the support of the overwhelming majority of unilingual Quebec francophones, and even of a very healthy 60% of the francophone majority at large. "Think back to everything that's happened since the 1960s," Ted said very loudly at one point: "we're just kidding ourselves when we pretend that these guys aren't going to win in the end." (And at this point Madeleine, whom I had very cleverly managed to sit beside, leaned over and whispered gently in my ear: "I remember when you said that last year, and I still think you're right.")

On the other hand (and the other hand again)

I was of course deeply pleased to discover that Madeleine thinks I am right about something. As I've already suggested, however (and did not exactly tell Madeleine the last time I was in Ottawa), I am not *altogether* certain that I am right myself.

One of the classic old pieces of folk wisdom about Canada is that it's a place which survives by never really trying to resolve its fundamental problems. (I can't remember the exact quotation, but I think this will do.) And at this exact moment in time I feel caught between two instincts in opposite directions.

On the one hand, this classic piece of folk wisdom strikes me as just a dusty artifact of the obsolete first self-governing dominion of the British empire. It is just another way of saying that the trouble with Canada, as the late Ontario premier, John Robarts, suggested when the Parti Québécois won its first Quebec provincial election in the fall of 1976, is that it has never quite decided whether or not it wants to exist.

Now, on this view, at the end of the twentieth century, the time has come for the people of Canada to make up their minds about whether they do want to be the people of Canada. And perhaps the history of the horrible conquest which none of us today can change has decided that the only practicable way for this to happen, in any foreseeable future, is through some new sovereignty-association arrangement between the first people who called themselves Canadians and the rest of us. And if this is true, there will in fact be another Quebec sovereignty referendum in the near enough future, and the Yes side will win by something in the order of 52% (or perhaps even a little more). And the rest of us will at last have a chance to see if we, too, do have what it takes to become a democratic people – our part of the people of Canada at large, if you like, ourselves alone – and all that.

On the other hand, perhaps my wife, who is a very down-to-earth person, is at least right about one thing, and a Yes-side victory in a next referendum is pie in the sky that is just not going to happen. In this case, the classic piece of folk wisdom about how Canada survives by never really trying to resolve its fundamental problems is not at all an artifact of the dusty old dominion. It is, instead, the truest and deepest message of the new legend of the fur trade, from coast to coast to coast. And, as a group of Canadian historians apparently told *Maclean's* magazine a while ago, the historic Canadian prime minister who comes closest to approximating a great leader is not Pierre Elliott Trudeau, but the incredible Canadian spiritualist, William Lyon Mackenzie King, whose motto was that he would make a decision if necessary but not necessarily a decision.

This, I think it's fair to say, is in fact the essential default-gospel of the present Canadian federal government. (And, even worse, I voted for this government myself in the 1997 election.)* And if this gospel is true, then I'd guess the most likely thing that is going to happen in the great debate about the future of Canada and Quebec is *essentially nothing at all*. Lucien Bouchard and the PQ may indeed win the next Quebec provincial election. But (and here I think my wife is wrong) they will find that the people of Quebec are so confused by the interminable obfuscations and

---

*In fairness to myself, I should point out that if there had been a party with a sovereignty-association platform similar to the one I have outlined earlier in this book, I would have voted for it, instead. But there is no such party in Canadian politics today. And it distresses me to think that, for practical purposes, that *may* just say everything which needs to be said.

vague threats of Jean Chrétien and his federal cabinet ministers – to say nothing of Preston Manning, Alexa McDonough, Jean Charest, Glen Clark, Ralph Klein, Roy Romanow, Mike Harris, Daniel Johnson, Brian Tobin, and the altogether amazing Gilles Duceppe – that they are no longer capable of making up *their* minds about anything else either. And so, shrewdly fearing that the good guys might lose a next referendum, Bouchard and the PQ will keep putting it off and putting it off, until almost everyone everywhere no longer cares.

The sovereign Quebec that already exists

If my last prediction here were to prove correct (and of course I am no more certain about this than anything else), then I think that the best advice for all of us who choose to be involved in the democratic debate about the future of Canada and Quebec would be to do nothing at all ourselves. And I think this advice ultimately makes sense for both those among "us" in the rest of the country, and those among us in Quebec.

As far as Quebec goes, Veronica is only half-right when she talks about some formal recognition of what it has actually become. Whatever formal recognition may mean, it doesn't put anything you can touch and feel in anyone's pocket – and very few of us ever get very much of it anyway. But I have been visiting Quebec for well over three decades now: ever since I first hitch-hiked to the Gaspé coast in 1963. And it seems indisputable to me that it has become something enormously different from what it was in the bad old days, through its own impressive exertions. For almost all practical purposes, the francophone majority now *is* "maîtres chez nous," just as the 1960s' quiet revolutionaries said it ought to be.

Quebec has had its own flag since as long ago as 1948 (a year after Ottawa finally created the legal status of a Canadian citizen). The separate Quebec Pension Plan of 1966 has funded the Caisse de dépôt et placement, which has in turn helped spawn a dynamic enough new francophone business class in the lower St. Lawrence valley. Ever since 1968, the provincial legislature, customarily known as the Legislative Assembly elsewhere in Canada, has been officially known as the Assemblée nationale in Quebec. Ever since 1977, Bill 101 has decreed that French is the only official language of Quebec. The sovereigntist Parti Québécois has served as the duly constituted provincial government of Quebec from 1976 to 1985, and from 1994 to the present.

In at least some significant senses, there already is a democratic people of Quebec, and within the division of powers prescribed in the Canadian federal constitution it is already "sovereign" as well.* Moreover, thanks in no small part to the influence of Quebec, the Canadian federal system is already notably decentralized in practice. And what the francophone democratic majority in Quebec has been able to achieve over the past generation is itself an impressive testimony to the relative autonomy and independent power that this system grants to the Assemblé nationale and democratic government of Quebec.

It is of course true that Quebec residents still pay taxes to both the government of Quebec in Quebec City, and the federal government of Canada in Ottawa. But Quebecers, like all other Canadians, receive federal benefits for the taxes they pay. As shown in some of the earlier statistical exhibits I've included in my reflections here, Quebec does not in fact benefit from federal transfers to quite the disproportionate extent that some in other parts of the country imagine.** But it does benefit disproportionately – certainly in a way that is not true of any of the other large provinces of Alberta, British Columbia, or Ontario. And, ever since Pierre Trudeau at least, for more than a few Quebecers the Canadian federal government has been a kind of dynamic growth industry in its own right. "For some 30 years," Lysiane Gagnon

---

*According to a 1914 study that Walt recently sent along in the mail, for instance: "Within the limitations prescribed by the British North America Act, the Province of Ontario is a sovereign state." And what "these limitations may be is a constitutional question which is pertinent to all the provinces of the Dominion." (And Walt says that if you want to check this, look in volume XVII of the 1914 edition of *Canada and Its Provinces*.)

**See Exhibits 27 and 28 (pp. 131–132). By the way, I've now decided that I'm going to put all my reflections here between covers, and send them along to Ted in Ottawa, whether he reads them or not.

acknowledged recently in a column in Canada's national newspaper, "Canada's politics have indeed been dominated by the Quebec agenda, and the country has lived for practically all that time under prime ministers from Quebec."

When you add all this up, it is not as if doing nothing at all in the great debate on the future of Canada and Quebec would mean ignoring egregious practical grievances or flagrant and outrageous injustices in Quebec. To no small extent, Quebec is already quite "sovereign" and quite "national" and, at the same time, highly influential in the Canadian federal system. If the choice ultimately is between holding yet another referendum that can't quite be won and doing nothing, even the sovereigntist movement may finally conclude that it's better if nothing happens at all.

The ominous fragility in the rest of Canada

Of course, I myself live in the rest of the country, not Quebec, and it is the rest of Canada that concerns me in the end. If Quebec sovereigntists can win some form of majority in a next referendum, then I do think that the rest of us will have no choice but to try to negotiate some form of sovereignty-association arrangement that will work for us as well as it works for Quebec. But if the sovereigntist movement can't do this, then I especially think that it is best for the rest of us to do nothing at all.

To me, the great trouble with what Veronica wants to do – to keep pressuring the rest of the country into some more moderate accommodation of the late twentieth-century sovereigntist impulse in Quebec – is that we've already reached the point where pressure of this sort has begun to eat away at the ties that bind the rest of the country to Canada itself. However you twist or turn it, as best as I can make out, you finally do come back to Trudeau's principle: it simply *is* an injustice to the rest of us to *both* give Quebec greater influence in the federal system at large and, at the same time, recognize (no matter how moderately) that it has some form of special status, which makes it not an "equal" province like the others, and entitles it not to "put Canada first" as all the other provinces must do.

Alas, this does seem to me exactly what Veronica, and Stéphane Dion and Daniel Johnson and Jean Charest and, most recently, even a few among the provincial premiers outside Quebec, finally want to try to do, yet again. And, in the eyes of too many people of Canada in the rest of the country, it only turns Canada into a mere hollow holding corporation for Quebec – a political enterprise whose overriding purpose and most fundamental objective is simply to keep on accommodating Quebec, so that the sovereigntist movement cannot make good on its threat to secede from the country. (And, by the way, I think this also goes some considerable distance towards explaining why the ancient question of Canadian annexation to the United States has lately become a more almost-serious subject in English-speaking Canada than at any other time I can remember.)

It is probably worth noting, yet again as well, that the crucial issue here does *not* turn around some vague or strictly symbolic recognition of Quebec's "unique character." Opinion polls suggest that substantial majorities in all parts of the country felt that the provincial premiers' gentle noises on this theme in the late summer of 1997 were a "positive step in right direction." But the Quebec Liberal Party quickly made clear that moderate accommodation must mean much more than this. The prominent pollster, Darrell Bricker, has explained that, even for the Meech Lake and Charlottetown Accords, early polls showed a similar popular support. It was only when "people found out some of the details" that "they started to back away."

In the same spirit, if there were some more moderate way of negotiating the partial withdrawal of Quebec from the Canadian federal system that I've discussed earlier – without another referendum in Quebec – then I do think this would be something worth trying to do. The decisive point here is that *for every degree that Quebec withdraws from the larger system, it also loses some commensurate degree of influence over the system's management and operation.* This is fair and just for the rest of the country, and directly addresses what seems to be the most fundamental problem in Quebec as well.

I would be cautiously optimistic myself if I thought there were any chance that the premiers outside Quebec might move further in this particular right direction. Politics being what it is, however, I suppose I can appreciate how no practical federalist politician could consider endorsing such a project – and all the comfortable applecarts it would inevitably upset, in Ottawa and virtually all the provincial capitals – without the unique and unavoidable political pressures that a Yes-side victory in a next referendum would bring.

Meanwhile, one principle the provincial premiers do seem to have agreed on is: *"If any future constitutional amendment confers powers on one province, these powers must be available to all provinces."** This principle, apparently, is the only way of ensuring justice and fairness for the rest of the country, without the dramatic shift in political climate wrought by a Yes-side victory in another Quebec sovereignty referendum. And, as a basis for negotiating any practical scheme of renewed federalism, that might actually satisfy some decisive majority among the democratic people and the assorted political elites of Quebec, it does seem to me ominously close to a recipe for the ultimate deconstruction of Canada itself.

And so the argument comes back to where it began. If there is not going to be another referendum, then it is best to do nothing at all. My own sense is that the events of the past few decades, culminating with the 1995 referendum in Quebec, have in fact created both a new kind of Canada and a new kind of Quebec. For the moment the highest-minded policy, in everyone's interest, just may be to let the dust settle, and to let the new waters that have begun to rise seek their own level. In a few decades it will be clearer to all of us what has really happened, and what is and what is not important. And then a new generation of political leadership will be able to start giving formal recognition to all the new realities – in Quebec *and* western Canada *and* Atlantic Canada *and* aboriginal Canada *and* Ontario and on and on – and finally in the Canada to which the multiracial northern fur trade gave birth, from coast to coast to coast.

---

*I am quoting from the report on the recent "Calgary declaration" (or whatever the correct name is) in the *Globe and Mail*, September 15, 1997, A4.

Exhibit 42
Emerging New Metropolitan Rivalries
in Ontario and Western Canada
Population Growth, 1921–1991

Year	Population (000s)		Cal-Ed-Van /
	Toronto	Cal-Ed-Van*	Toronto
1921	686	389	.57
1931	**901**	**557**	**.62**
1941	1,002	642	.64
1951	**1,264**	**929**	**.73**
1961	1,919	1,466	.76
1971	**2,628**	**1,981**	**.75**
1981	2,999	2,518	.84
1991	**4,036**	**3,274**	**.81**

*Combined population of Calgary, Edmonton, and Vancouver metropolitan areas.

SOURCE: Statistics Canada.

32

Two False Paths
in the Northern Wilderness

It is sometimes said that Canadians have clear ideas about what they do *not* want to be, but only the vaguest of notions about what they are or want to become. This is usually meant as a criticism, and in certain respects it certainly is. Yet when you think about all the peculiar circumstances of Canada, it isn't so surprising that it should be a place which reaches to define itself by just saying what it is not, and then (as it were) lets its people become whatever else they may choose themselves.

A strategy of this type does have obvious limitations. Yet it may also be one sensible enough part of some wider approach to expanding the realm of human freedom in the challenging new global village of the twenty-first century. And when I'm prompted to contemplate what I value most about Canada (as I am right now, by the imminent end of all my reflections here), it does occur to me that it has a lot to do with the very last word in that trite phrase from what currently passes for an English-language Canadian national anthem – "the true north, strong and *free*."

It seems to me that, if you put your mind to it, you can still live an unusually free life in Canada. (And this is what is ultimately meant, I think, when the United Nations surveys keep on reporting that Canada is the best country in the world in which to live.) Canada's unique freedom, many would rush to point out, is largely the result of a historical accident, rather than any grand design. But even if you only accidentally stumble on something that is valuable, that doesn't mean you should give it up.

In any case, as an epilogue of sorts to everything I've written down so far, I have two utterly final thoughts about particular things we ought *not* to do over the next few decades, if we do value the kind of life that Canada has been able to provide in our own generations – and if we really want to try to do something to ensure that Canada can keep on providing this kind of life, for generations upon generations upon generations to come.

Radical decentralization

I have already hinted broadly at the first particular thing I don't think we should do, when I commented a few pages ago on the anglophone provincial premiers' recently enunciated principle: "If any future constitutional amendment confers powers on one province, these powers must be available to all provinces."

By way of background here, I should probably confess what may already be obvious enough: that the part of the rest of Canada I live in myself is Ontario. And, through some unconscious process of osmosis, I have no doubt wound up with a few attitudes that at least used to be thought typical of central Canadians. (I say "used to be" because I'm not sure just what Mike Harris is doing, and it sometimes seems to me that whatever it is may not be so typical of the past I know, though I'm not sure about this, or at all sure that Mike Harris himself knows either.)

At the same time, I also want to stress that I did not have much trouble understanding what Senator Pat Carney was driving at, when she recently urged, in so many words, that British Columbia has just as much right to secede from Canada as Quebec. And while (just like 57% of the federal electorate in BC in the 1997 election) I would not vote for Preston Manning myself, I think he has already made some useful contributions to public debate in Canada. And I certainly respect the maturing western Canadian power and protest that his election as leader of the official opposition in 1997 might be said to symbolize.

I am all for provincial rights as well. I am a great admirer of the unfortunately somewhat obscure nineteenth-century Ontario Liberal premier, Oliver Mowat, whose now largely forgotten struggles with John A. Macdonald did so much to inaugurate the tradition of "province building" in Canadian politics. And I think a lot of what is too often criticized as regionalism in Canada really is, as Harold Innis shrewdly observed more than a half-century ago, a source of Canadian national strength. (Strong provinces, in Innis's own words, have been "nuclei of defence" against the harsh pressures with which Canada has always had to struggle in its North American continental environment.)

Having said all this, however, I think that Preston Manning's *radically* decentralizing vision of a "new federalism" (or what he himself has christened "Plan C") is most definitely something that the people of Canada should *not* be experimenting with in the twenty-first century. And this is equally true of the somewhat different but essentially (and rather ironically) parallel visions of radical decentralization, which have bubbled up among the troubled waters of renewed federalism in such central Canadian places as Montreal and Kingston over the past number of years.

Again, in the most recent past (as I write, in any case), the picture here has been confused by the provincial premiers' apparent endorsement of the principle that new powers extended to any one province must be available to all other provinces. Manning seems to see this as something of an endorsement of his decentralizing vision. And with the federal government also making vague warm noises about the premiers' initiative, some say that virtually all Canadian politicians outside the Quebec sovereigntist movement are now tilting in this direction.[*] It strikes me that there are a lot of political shell games going on here. Yet even if all the politicians were to favour some form of radical decentralization, my own view is that they would all be wrong.

A "strong national community"

For the time being, I am not too worried. Some 84% of Canada's population today lives in the four large provinces of Ontario, Quebec, British Columbia, and Alberta. Six of Canada's present ten provinces, in other words, just don't have at all enough demographic weight to take advantage of "giving all provinces more powers," even if they find the concept attractive from other points of view. And if each "equal" province has one vote in deciding on such things, as the theory would suggest it ought to, the majority of provinces are bound to vote against any serious radical decentralization of the Canadian federal system.

Over the longer term, on the other hand, one might reason-

---

[*]Or, in terms of the so-called plans, Manning's "Plan C" has now been folded into the more mainstream "Plans A and B." In fact, I am particularly confused about all this at the moment, and I think I have a right to be.

ably wonder how long governments supposedly representing 16% of the Canada-wide population can prevail against the wishes of governments supposedly representing the other 84%. Here it seems to me that there is a still more fundamental problem. And I think it is worth worrying about quite a lot. If you look around at what is actually happening in the dynamic global village (as opposed to what certain wild prophets in the media say), financial globalization, the microelectronics revolution, the information age, and all that, are making an at least suitably up-to-date version of the national state *more*, not less important in world history – at least from the standpoint of the vast majority of democratic peoples everywhere.

In this setting, it seems to me, the people of Canada (as opposed to the people of Quebec) would increasingly find that they were missing something in a radically decentralized confederation, which reduced the role of the only national government they have to that of a kind of scorekeeper at interprovincial conferences. And, even though it might go against all their deepest preferences and inclinations, they would ultimately find themselves looking for what they are missing in Canada elsewhere. And of course the closest place to find such a thing would be in the still resolutely national state of the USA.

Happily enough in this case as well, I often think that even Preston Manning, if he ever were to become prime minister of Canada, would prove less interested in radically decentralizing the federation than he says he is now (just as he proved more interested in living in the official opposition leader's official house at Stornaway, perhaps). In any event, Ted has also sent me a copy of a passage from a recent book by University of Calgary professor, Roger Gibbins, and his colleague, Sonia Arrison. And it has bolstered my underlying Canada-wide faith that radical decentralization is *not* really what the great new wind from the west is finally all about. In fact, Gibbins and Arrison tell us, western Canadians

> have always believed in a strong, national community. A Canada that has been gutted of any clear sense of collective purpose, that has been radically decentralized in an effort to appease nationalist forces in Quebec, and that no longer has the financial resources or political will to pursue national social programs – such a Canada

would be of limited interest to western Canadians.*

The rise of the American empire

Of course, as these concerns about just where radical decentralization of the Canadian federation could lead themselves imply, the one great thing English-speaking (and even, I think, French-speaking) Canadians (or even Québécois) have always been certain they did *not* want to be is citizens of the USA.

Of course, as well, the conventional sophisticated observation on this preference today is that it is childish and negative and Freudian, and so on. But I think this sort of criticism misses the deepest truth. It is ultimately because Canadians really are so "American" that they do not want to be citizens of the USA.

To start with, I believe myself that the real danger for Canada in its present circumstances is not quite annexation to or by the USA itself. As is often-enough observed, there are good reasons for suspecting that even the present US political system would not exactly want to swallow this kind of prospect.

Thus *Business Week* magazine in New York recently noted polling data showing that Canadians (including, apparently, a great many domestic supporters of Preston Manning, Ralph Klein, Mike Harris, and so forth) would overwhelmingly vote for the Democratic Party in US elections. Nine or even ten new Canadian states of the union, the magazine quietly implied, could almost guarantee Democratic domination of both the Presidency and the Senate in Washington for who knows how long to come. And, for the time being in any case, this gives assorted influential Americans excellent reasons for opposing any form of outright US annexation of Canadian provinces.**

What is probably the much more likely prospect in this connection was rather broadly hinted at in an article on Canada

---

*Cited, Ted notes, in *Canada Opinion, A newsletter published by The Council for Canadian Unity*, April 1996, 6.

**And "for the time being" here could mean a rather long while. Walt has also pointed out to me that, as long ago as 1955, the Canadian historian and political activist, Frank Underhill, observed: "practically all Canadians, of course, vote Democratic in American elections."

which appeared in the influential US policy journal, *Foreign Affairs*, not too long after the October 1995 referendum in Quebec. I haven't read this article myself, but I've talked about it with Walt over the phone. The thrust of the piece, Walt says, is that if Quebec were to become independent, the US might find itself suddenly burdened with the remaining Canadian provinces. And the way to go would be to leave the present Canadian system intact for purposes of domestic government and politics, while transferring the lion's share of responsibility for Canada's foreign and defence policy and whatnot to Washington.*

Logically enough, Walt notes ("from some points of view"), this scenario bears some striking resemblances to the circumstances of the old first self-governing dominion of the British empire. Walt, in fact, believes that a vague, half-mindless drift towards a new status as some form of first self-governing dominion of an American global empire is also probably the greatest real danger for the future of Canada today – regardless of what may or may not happen in Quebec.

He urges as well that the drift in this direction is all the more "dangerous" (so to speak), because it is something with which so many old traditions of leadership in English-speaking Canada are quite comfortable. If, for the sake of convenience, you take the new maple leaf flag of 1965 as the decisive turning point, for some three-quarters of the time that the Canadian confederation of 1867 has now been around it *has* in fact been a merely self-governing dominion of someone else's empire, and not a democratic national state in its own right. And, to no small extent, Canada remained in these circumstances for as long as it did because so many traditional English-speaking Canadian leaders more or less liked things that way.

Moreover, the traditions of leadership involved, I think myself, are not altogether without virtue (perhaps especially in the turbulent new age of the global village that already seems to be upon us now). And I would agree with Walt that these old traditions – suitably updated for the twenty-first century, when

---

*Walt did give me a reference here, which I still haven't had time to check out myself: Charles F. Doran, "Will Canada Unravel?" *Foreign Affairs*, September-October 1996, 97–109.

Harold Innis's "change from British imperialism to American imperialism" in Canada has progressed far beyond any conceivable point of return – *have* lately become stronger than they have been for all but the very early parts of my own Canadian life.

The Canadian democracy in America today

In the USA as well, there have lately been some signs of a new willingness to embrace the destiny of inheriting the old English-speaking empire on which the sun never set, at least somewhat more explicitly and openly than in the past.

("Isn't it intriguing," Madeleine said to me over the phone a few weeks after the tragic death of Princess Diana in France, "how some parts of the US mass media more and more seem to be treating the UK Royal Family as a kind of US Royal Family, too?" And I had to agree with her that I thought it was.)

As Walt also says, however, "Canada is above all else an ironic place." And ironically enough, it *is* the American who does lurk inside every Canadian who most strongly urges us to resist the drift towards some new Canadian status as the first self-governing dominion of some new and more grand and noble anglo-American global empire, in the age of television, high technology, and rock and roll.

From Sam Slick to William Lyon Mackenzie to Louis Riel to William Lyon Mackenzie King to the majority who vainly voted against Canada-US free trade in the 1988 federal election to Glen Clark and the BC fishers, it is the American inside us who has struggled to grow beyond the old dominion status. (And whatever else one might want to say about Glen Clark and the BC fishers, they *have* lately stood up courageously for the rights of the aspiring new national democracy, on Canada's Pacific Coast – with very little help or even encouragement from Canada's "national" government in Ottawa. And, as Walt has lately reminded me as well, as long ago as 1938 the almost alarmingly prescient Harold Innis was urging just how important it is for Canada to stand on guard against "the narrowness of interest in which it may be advantageous ... for American interests to prevent measures which may lead to conservation of resources, as in the British Columbia salmon fishery.")

It has also been our own most friendly American democratic advisors who have always urged us to cast aside the obsolete empire and become a proper new-world democratic country in our own right. Whatever may or may not finally happen in the current great and greatly aggravating debate on the future of Canada and Quebec, I think this is still by far the best advice. And my own hope is that we in Canada will just keep on following the advice of our most friendly American democratic national advisors, to the ends of the earth and the universe beyond. That, it seems to me at least, is how we can best show *our* faith in democracy in America, and in our common continental manifest destiny and historic progressive fate, and on and on and on.

Of course, I have no idea if this is what will actually happen. In this, as in other respects, there are probably a few too many senses in which I remain somewhat confused. But I think I may actually have started to figure out what I'd like to see happen myself. And I've decided to take this as an optimistic sign.

Exhibit 43
Canada and Its Ten Equal Provinces Today
Population (000s), 1996

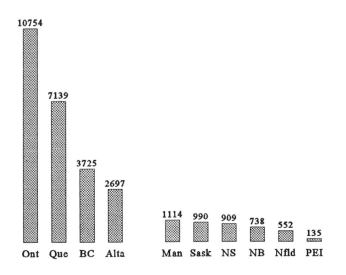

SOURCE: Statistics Canada.

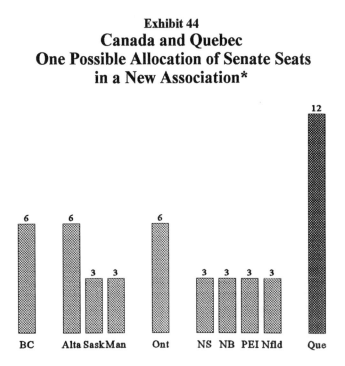

Exhibit 44
Canada and Quebec
One Possible Allocation of Senate Seats
in a New Association*

*As explained in Part Nine, on this scenario a "sovereign Quebec" would have no seats in what is presently known as the House of Commons, and its twelve senators would be "part-time," with responsibility only for those functions of government with respect to which the people of Quebec remained part of the people of Canada.

Index

Abbott, John, 197
Aboriginal peoples of Canada, 15, 16, 69, 71-72, 75-76, 114, 116, 141, 150-151, 153-158, 173-176, 194, 223
Aboriginal self-government, 17, 25, 155-156
Acadians, 46, 159
Alberta, 18, 96-97, 102, 107, 115, 123-124, 130-131, 134, 142-143, 148, 195, 209, 211-212, 220, 227
Algonquin, 155, 157
Allophones, 44-45
Amending formula for Canadian constitution, 82, 195
American Civil War, 55
American empire, 53, 70, 122, 126, 138, 229-232
American War of Independence, 63, 64, 167-168
Annexation of Canada to US, 27-29, 34, 145, 222
Armed force after Yes victory in Quebec referendum, 185-186
Arrison, Sonia, 228
Asia-Pacific region, 8, 111, 144
Assemblée nationale, 197, 201-202, 220
Assembly of First Nations, 156
Assiniboine, 155, 157
Atlantic Canada, 17, 46, 115-116, 130-131, 137-138, 142-144, 146, 159, 205, 211, 223
Automobile industry, 101-104, 108-109

Balancing the budget, 9, 22, 110-111
Bilingualism, 13, 14, 39-42, 46-50, 76-78, 162
Blair, Tony, 170
Bloc Québécois, 21-22, 164
Bloskie, C., 97, 108
Bothwell, Robert, 42
Bouchard, Audrey, 22
Bouchard, Lucien, 21-22, 70, 161, 181-183, 218-219
Bourassa, Henri, 163
Bourassa, Robert, 15, 17
Bourgault, Pierre, 10
Bre-X, 97-98
Bricker, Darrell, 222

British Columbia, 18, 38, 65, 87, 102, 106, 114-115, 123-124, 130-131, 134, 142-143, 148, 195, 208-212, 220, 226-227
British Columbia salmon fishery, 231-232
British conquest of Canada (la conquête), 51-55, 62, 166-167
British empire (and Commonwealth of Nations), 59, 60, 63, 66, 67, 69, 77, 80-82, 85, 120-122, 126, 138, 146, 167-171, 173, 217, 231
British North America Act (see Constitution Act, 1867)
Business Week magazine, 229

Caisse de dépôt et placement du Québec, 89, 219
Calgary, 64, 136, 141, 174, 177, 196, 228
Calgary declaration, 223
California, 26, 30, 54, 209
Canada as an aboriginal word, 159
Canada Day (Dominion Day), 60
Canada Pension Plan, 89-91
Canada-US Trade Agreement 1989 (FTA), 26-27, 103, 120, 231
Canadian Arctic, 155-156
Canadian business leaders, 145
Canadian Charter of Rights and Freedoms, 15
Canadian economic space, 137, 143-144, 212
Canadian federal election 1997, 11, 22, 53, 115, 163-164, 183, 187, 191, 194, 203, 215, 218
Canadian flag, 86-88, 125, 230
Canadian Historical Association, 137
Canadian House of Commons, 196, 198, 206, 208, 234
Canadian national railway system, 32, 118, 120, 176
Canadian Shield, 123
Canoe and portage, 32-34, 39, 70, 75-76, 118
Carney, Pat, 226
Cartier, Georges-Étienne, 162-163, 175
Charest, Jean, 186-188, 202, 219, 222
Charlottetown Accord, 16-19, 21, 26, 34, 156, 194-195, 222

Chile and Canada, trade agreement, 27
Chipewyan, 155, 157
Chrétien, Jean, 22, 25, 27, 184, 199, 202, 219
Citizenship Act 1947, 80-81, 169
Citizenship Act 1977, 81, 169
Clark, Glen, 219, 231
Clinton, Bill, 170
Common-law unions in Quebec and rest of Canada, 203-204
Communication in a democracy, 160-162, 207
Computer technology, 14, 32, 108-109, 151
Confederation debates 1865, 175, 177
Constitution Act, 1867, 16, 39, 82, 159, 171
Constitution Act, 1982, 15, 82, 127, 129, 154, 159
Council for Canadian Unity, 229
Craig, G.M., 65
Cree, 16, 77, 155, 157, 174
Creighton, Donald, 116-118, 122
Crosbie, John, 33
Cross, P., 97, 108

Dales, John H., 95
Davies, Robertson, 66
Democracy, 13-14, 34-35, 39-40, 52-53, 59-60, 66, 81, 88, 128, 146-147, 151, 160-161, 184-185, 202, 207, 220, 231-232
Democratic national state in Canada, 60, 61, 69, 74-78, 80-91, 125, 162-164, 171, 230-232
Deschamps, Yvon, 16
Diefenbaker, John, 90
Dion, Leon, 186, 200
Dion, Stéphane, 200, 202, 222
Dissatisfaction in Canada, 198, 214
Distinct society in Quebec, 15-17, 26
Division of Canada's national debt, 199
Dominion of Canada, 59, 60, 62, 65, 66, 69, 71, 74, 77-78, 80, 125, 129, 159, 162-163, 167, 169-170, 177, 197, 218, 230
Dominion status in British empire, 85
Doran, Charles, 230
Downsizing, 110
Duceppe, Gilles, 219
Dumont, Mario, 21

East-west economy, 101, 117-118, 121-125, 136-138, 142-144
Edmonton, 116, 174
English-speaking Canada, 23-25, 41, 48, 64-66, 77-78, 166-172, 205
Equal partnership in sovereignty-association, 191-192, 203
Equality of provinces, 206-207, 221, 227, 233
Equalization payments, 116, 127-132, 211-212
Ethnic origin, 61, 78, 172
Export base, 97, 99-100, 105-108, 111-112, 126

Federal transfers to provincial governments, 132, 220
Financial impact of Yes victory in Quebec referendum, 187-188
Financial sector, 97-98, 141
First identity in Canadian provinces and regions, 165
Fishing industry, 95, 231-232
Fontaine, Phil, 156
Foreign Affairs, 230
Founding peoples, 64, 75-76, 159
Fowke, Vernon, 95
France, role in Quebec politics, 24-25, 202
Francis, Diane, 53, 145
Francophone business class in Quebec, 89-90, 109, 124, 136-137, 145
Francophone majority in Quebec, 16, 40, 45-47, 54-55, 58, 60, 91, 116, 136, 160, 164, 217, 220
French and English cultural antagonism, 52
French as a doomed language, debate on, 53-56
French empire in America, 77, 120, 173
French language rights outside Quebec, early history, 39, 52
French Revolution, 63
Front de libération du Québec (FLQ), 8-10, 185
Frum, Barbara, 15-16
Fur trade in Canada (and fur trade legend), 39, 65, 69-78, 89, 94-95, 116-118, 125, 153, 159, 166, 170-171, 173-178, 223

Index

Gagnon, Lysiane, 192, 221
Geography, 12, 30-36, 38-39, 43, 69-78, 122-124, 128-129, 138, 146, 150-151, 153, 157, 160-162, 205
Gérin-Lajoie, Paul, 9, 10
Gibbins, Roger, 228
Globalization, 9, 13, 32, 53, 108-110, 157, 228
Globe (Globe and Mail), 59, 191-192, 223
Government as monopoly of legitimate force, 151, 185
Government intervention in economic life, 110-112, 120
Governor General of Canada, 83-84
Great Spirit of Canada, 27, 34, 77, 157
Grégoire, Gilles, 10
Guthrie, J.A., 95
Gwyn, Richard, 41

Haida, 155, 157, 174
Halifax, 141
Hanson, Eric J., 95
Harper, Elijah, 16
Harris, Mike, 211, 219, 226, 229
Harris, R. Cole, 71, 117
Health care system in Canada, 34, 88-89, 134
Hockey in Canada, 30
Hoffman, Arnold, 95
Holiday, Billie, 176
Hollywood movie industry, 66
Hudson's Bay Company, 64, 76, 77, 86, 122, 166-167
Huron, 141, 155, 157
Hurtig, Mel, 116
Hydroelectricity, 95, 123

Ice age in Canada, 32, 71
Immigration, 13, 30, 64-68, 73, 76, 169-171, 176-178
Imperial Preference, 121
Innis, Harold, 70- 72, 75, 77, 87, 95, 102, 116-117, 121-123, 125, 127, 130, 138, 141, 153-154, 170, 176, 210, 226, 231-232
Inuit, 153-157
Iroquois, 141, 155, 157, 174

Japanese branch plants, 108-109
Jesuits from France, 72
Johnson, Daniel, 219, 222
Jonquière, 35

Judicial Committee of the Privy Council, 82

Kelley, Jane H., 74
Kemper, Margaret Sinclair Trudeau, 38
King, William Lyon Mackenzie, 38, 218, 231
Kingston, 227
Kitchener, 174
Klein, Ralph, 219, 229
Knowledge of official languages, 46-50
Kootenay, 155, 157
Kwakiutl, 155, 157

Labour force in Canada, 96, 98, 104, 109-110
Landry, Bernard, 161
Laporte, Pierre, 10
Latin American trade with Canada, 111, 144
Laurentian thesis, 116-127, 129-130, 134, 147, 153, 210
Laurier, Wilfrid, 163, 175
Legality of Quebec secession, 184
Lesage, Jean, 10, 90
Lévesque, René, 10, 11, 15, 16, 91, 94, 137, 185, 190
Liberal Party of Canada, 10, 27, 87, 90, 203
Lincoln, Abraham, 55
Lobsters in the pot, 24, 202
Lotbinière, Henri Joly de, 175, 177
Louisiana, 46
Lower, Arthur, 70, 77, 78, 95, 137, 196
Lumbering, 95

Macdonald, John A., 120, 127, 144, 163, 175, 226
Mackenzie, William Lyon, 231
Maclean's magazine, 16, 38, 218
Manitoba, 16, 18, 65, 87, 101, 142-143, 201, 209, 211
Manning, Preston, 177, 219, 226-229
Manufacturing sector, 101-104, 108, 121, 124
Maple leaf as Canadian national symbol, 87-88
Maple Leaf Forever, 62
Marshall, Herbert, 102
Martin, Paul, 201
Massey, Vincent, 83-84
Matthews, Geoffrey, 71
McCall, Bruce, 167

McDonough, Alexa, 219
McKillop, A. Brian, 117
McLuhan, Marshall, 70, 117
Meech Lake Accord, 15-17, 31, 42, 51, 81, 90, 114-115, 185, 193, 196, 203, 216, 222
Métis, 153-155, 176, 178
Metropolitan centres in Canada, 73, 119, 140, 224
Mexico, 27, 120
Micmac, 155, 157, 174
Middle ground, 173
Mining in Canada, 95, 123
Montreal, 9-11, 21, 24, 41-42, 51, 97, 117-118, 123, 134-136,163, 174, 176-177, 201, 208, 227
Montreal Gazette, 135
Morse, Eric, 39, 43, 74
Mother tongue, 39, 44-46, 58
Movement souveraineté-association (MSA), 10
Mowat, Oliver, 226
Mulroney, Brian, 15, 16, 21
Multiculturalism, 17, 75-76, 159, 173-178, 223
Multilateral Agreement on Investment (MAI), 120
Multiple origins, 177-178

Nahani, 155
National business class, 134-140, 145-147
National Policy, 120, 127, 144
National treatment, 146
Nationalist tradition in French Canada, 10, 25
Negotiated secession of Quebec, 199, 201-204
New Brunswick, 46, 64-65, 201
New York State, 209
Newfoundland, 16, 33, 82-83, 87, 95, 116, 184, 187
Non-geographic communities, 151
Norse voyages to northern North America, 69
North American Free Trade Agreement 1994 (NAFTA), 27, 120
North West Company, 76, 77, 85, 118, 174
Northern Canada, 116, 144
Northern lights, 72
Northern Quebec, 116, 200-201
Northwest Territories, 155
Nova Scotia, 101, 122, 129, 168

Nunavut, 155-157

October Crisis, 10
Official languages of Canada, 15, 48, 91, 159
Oil and natural gas industry, 95-96
Oka, 185
Ontario, 46, 65, 87, 101-104, 106, 116, 121, 123-124, 130-131, 137-138, 142-144, 148, 159, 201, 206-212, 220, 223, 226-227
Ottawa (Ottawa-Hull), 13, 15, 48, 76, 177
Outremont, 186

Panama Canal, 122, 123
Parizeau, Jacques, 21, 24, 161, 182, 202
Parks Canada, 74
Parti Québécois (PQ), 10, 11, 14, 15, 21, 22, 46, 91, 137, 181-187, 190-193, 195, 202, 207, 216-220
Partial withdrawal, and partition, 200-201
Partial withdrawal, of other provinces, 206-207
Partial withdrawal, of Quebec from Canadian federal system, 192-198, 205, 222-223
Partition after Yes vote in Quebec referendum, 199-201
Patriation of Canadian constitution, 15, 94
"Peace, order, and good government," 171
Pearson, Lester, 87, 88, 90
People of Canada, 34, 146-147, 149-178, 193-194, 197, 211, 228, 234
People of Quebec, 160-162, 193-194, 228, 234
Pérusse, D., 97, 108
Plains Cree, 155, 157
Plans A, B, C, and D, 191, 227
Population in Canada, 12, 26, 30, 54, 84, 92, 189, 233, 207-212
Prairie provinces, 65, 95, 142, 177
Prime minister of Canada under sovereignty-association, 197-198
Prince Edward Island, 128, 143
Principle of powers available to all provinces, 223, 226
Province building in Canada, 226
Pulp and paper industry, 95, 123

Quebec economy, 101-104, 107, 121, 123-124, 130-131, 136-138, 142-144
Quebec flag, 219
Quebec Liberal Party, 10, 15, 17, 21, 216, 222
Quebec Pension Plan, 89-91, 109, 219
Quebec provincial elections, 10-11, 14-15, 21, 217
Quebec Reform Party, 163
Quebec representation in reformed Senate, 197, 211-212, 234
Québécois as resident of Quebec City, 163

Racism, 175-176
Radical decentralization, 190, 226-229
Radio, 15, 122
Radio-Canada, 162
Ralliement National (RN), 10
Rassemblement pour l'indépendance national (RIN), 10
Realignment of Canadian economic system, 121, 122, 125, 134, 138, 141-147
Realignment of national economic policy, 125, 134, 144-147, 181, 212
Red River settlement, 65
Referendum, Canada, October 1992, 17-20, 80
Referendum, law in Quebec, 22
Referendum, Newfoundland, 1948, 83
Referendum, Quebec, May 1980, 8, 15, 20, 38, 191
Referendum, Quebec, October 1995, 11, 20, 21, 23-25, 35, 38, 40, 41, 45, 51, 53, 160-161, 164, 182-183, 191, 215-219, 223
Referendum to confirm new Canada-Quebec deal, 195-196, 203
Regional alienation, 115-116, 118, 120, 123, 208
Renewed federalism, 182, 190, 216-217, 222-223, 227
Resnick, Philip, 193
Resource economy in Canada, 94-100, 101-102, 108-109, 116-118, 124, 210
Riel, Louis, 231
Robarts, John, 217
Roman Catholic church in Quebec, 63-64, 163
Romanow, Roy, 219
Roosevelt, Theodore, 122

Roy, F., 97, 108
Royal Canadian Mounted Police, 96
Royal Commission on Bilingualism and Biculturalism, 90-91
Russian Federation (former USSR), 30, 194

Saskatchewan, 33, 88, 209, 211
Self-employment, 110
Senate reform, 17, 25, 197, 211-212, 234
Service industry in Canada, 109-110
Seven Years' War, 62
Siegfried, André, 169
Simeon, Richard, 90
Simultaneous translation, 162
Slick, Sam, 231
Small business in Canada, 110
Social policy, 111, 127, 134, 144, 188, 228
Southard, Frank Jr., 102
Sovereignty of all Canadian provinces, 220
Sovereignty-association (partnership), 10, 20, 22, 24, 64, 181-182, 190-201, 215, 217-218, 234
St. Laurent, Gilles, 163
St. Laurent, Louis, 84, 163
Staples thesis, 96-97, 116-118
Statute of Westminster, 82-83, 85
Supranational structure in European Union, 192
Supreme Court of Canada, 82, 184

Taxation issue in sovereign Quebec, 184, 186, 196
Taylor, Kenneth W., 102
Team Canada trade missions, 22
Telecommunications industry in Canada, 109
Television, 14-15, 16, 24, 26, 42, 55, 85-86, 91, 168, 202
Territorial integrity of Quebec, 161
Texas, as Mexican province, 65
Thompson, David, 85
Thorsell, William, 191
Thunder Bay, 76
Tobin, Brian, 219
Toronto, 97, 114, 117-118, 136-138, 141, 173-175, 177, 208
Toronto-Ottawa-Montreal triangle, 115, 118, 127
Tough love, 58
Trevelyan, G.M., 167

Trigger, Bruce, 72
Trucking statistics, 136-139, 141-144, 147-148
Trudeau, Pierre, 10, 13, 15, 16, 22, 38-43, 46-48, 51, 53, 58, 74-78, 80-82, 90-91, 94, 110-111, 127, 154, 162-163, 199, 218, 220
Trudeau's position on special status for Quebec, 16, 90, 221
Turner, Frederick Jackson, 118
Two linguistic majorities in Canada, 53, 58, 160-162, 202, 207

UK Royal Family in US, 231
Underhill, Frank H., 175, 229
Unilateral declaration of independence, 182-186, 190
Unilingual anglophones and franco-phones, 35, 46-49, 51, 58, 215
Unique character of Quebec, 190, 222
United Empire Loyalists (and loyalist mythology), 63-67, 69, 74, 168-172
United Nations, 31, 194, 225
United States and Canada, 26, 27, 60, 63-65, 70, 102-103, 105, 111, 120-122, 143, 145, 147, 167-171, 176, 186, 204, 209-210, 229-232, 228
Usher, Dan, 128, 131-132

Vallières, Pierre, 163
Van Kirk, Sylvia, 71, 176
Vancouver, 38, 97, 114-115, 123, 141, 173-175, 177
Victoria, 174
Virtual reality, 32-33
Voter turnout in Canadian federal elections, 152

Waite, P.B., 59
War of 1812, 65
Wells, Clyde, 16
Westell, Anthony, 193
Western Canada, 17, 65, 74, 95-96, 115-116, 123, 130-131, 137-138, 142-144, 167, 177, 223, 228-229
Westminster model, 169
Westmount, 9, 186
Williams, Glen, 103
Williamson, Ronald F., 74
Wilson, Edmund, 170
Wilson, Gordon, 208
Winnipeg, 128, 141, 174, 177, 209
Women's issues, 17, 71, 176
World languages, 53-56
World Trade Organization (WTO), 120
World's largest national economies, 180
Wright, Ronald, 154